The Musings of an Old Imperfect Christian

By Alec Hall

Copyright © 2018 Alec Hall

ISBN: 978-1-60383-566-4

Published by:
Holy Fire Publishing
www.HolyFirePublishing.com

Cover Design: Vanessa Hensel

Printed in the United States of America, The United Kingdom and Australia

To Diane and all our wonderful families

Introduction:

The following is a collection of my short writings, opinions, beliefs plus a few glimpses into the lives of some of our saints and characters. I cannot say that it is all original, as many people have influenced my life, some, I'm afraid I am ashamed to say, I have forgotten. I must mention though William Barclay, Nicky Gumbel, J.W.C. Wand, Derek Nimmo (Epitaphs), Encyclopaedia Britannica and countless others.

The topics are quite varied. I feel that readers will be able to dip in and out at their fancy but I do hope that something will be of use mainly to help us all to live the Christian life more perfectly in the power of the Holy Spirit.

I would not expect everyone to agree with all my opinions but maybe some subjects could stimulate profitable discussion. It might be helpful to have a Bible to hand now and again as some readings are quite long.

Background of author

Alec's working life was mainly in retail banking though the last twenty years were spent as a lecture and then a senior lecturer in banking with the last nine of those years as Deputy Head of Business and Management in a college. He has been retired over twenty years which has enabled him to work more as a volunteer for the Salvation Army (S.A.) of which he has been a member most of his life. His parents and grandparents were Salvationists, in fact his dad's father was an officer in the early days of the S.A. who was imprisoned for fourteen days for causing a disturbance of the peace. In those days, some of the magistrates were anti-Army because of their stand against alcohol. Hence, the author has a dodgy background!

Table of Contents

Chapter 1
Reasons why I believe

The following account was motivated by a well-known illusionist who wrote some time ago to the Independent with his 'Five reasons I stopped believing in God'. Readers were invited to respond with their lists. I did, outlining my ten reasons why I still believed in God. Alas, they were not printed! Since then I have given more consideration to my reasons and they follow because Peter says that Christians should always be prepared to give an answer to everyone who asks them to give a reason for the hope that they have.

1. The New Testament. The preface to the New International Version of the Bible says: 'No other piece of ancient literature has an abundance of manuscript witnesses as does the New Testament'. It is believed that the New Testament was originally written between AD 40 and 100 with a full manuscript of the whole New Testament from as early as AD 350. There are over 5,000 Greek manuscripts, over 10,000 Latin Manuscripts and 9,300 other manuscripts. F.J.A. Hort, one of the greatest textual critics, says: 'In the variety and fullness of the evidence on which it rests, the text of the New Testament stands absolutely and unapproachably alone among ancient prose writings.' We can say that no other book has been exposed to the critical research that the Bible has suffered, and, not just by unbelievers. Compare that with evidence of other events. For Caesar's Gallic wars, we have 9 or 10 copies of the history, the oldest

being written 900 years after the event. We have only 20 copies of the work of Tacitus. Yet no scholar doubts the authenticity of these works.

So, how long after the recorded events was the New Testament written? Was it years before the events were put on paper? The answer is no.

Peter says, 'We did not follow cleverly invented stories when we told you about the power and coming of our Lord Jesus Christ but we were eyewitnesses of His majesty.....We ourselves heard this voice that came from heaven.....' (2 Peter ch 1 v 16,17) and another eyewitness, John says: 'That which was from the beginning, which we have heard, which we have seen with our eyes, which we have looked at and our hands have touched...' (1 John ch 1 v 1) Another, Paul: 'He appeared to Peter, and then to the twelve. After that, He appeared to more than five hundred of the brothers at the same time....then he appeared to James, then to all the apostles and last of all He appeared to me....' (1 Corinthians~ ch 15). The four gospels were written by Matthew, Mark, and John all disciples of Jesus' day. Luke followed after, companion of Paul, a revered historian, an educated man. It is believed that Luke travelled extensively around Palestine, that he interviewed close relations of Jesus. How else could he have recorded such personal details of Mary and others? The Acts of the Apostles, also written by Luke, include personal accounts, referred to as the 'we' chapters, when Luke was present.

12

Richard Dawkins wrote a book called The God Delusion in 2006. He is allegedly 'one of the top three intellectuals in the world today'. On page 5, he writes: 'If this book works as 1 intend, religious readers who open it will be atheists when they put it down'. In ch. 3 called 'Arguments for God's existence', he has a heading The Arguments from Scripture, after 5 pages, he writes: 'I shall not consider the Bible further as evidence for any kind of deity'. He uses completely unreliable data which Dan Brown used in the fictional Da Vinci Code. Although amazingly many praise his book, there are serious critics who include atheists who are not happy with his approach. Alister McGrath once an atheist, now a Christian, has a doctorate in molecular biophysics, and has written a book called 'The Dawkins Delusion'. Here is a brief quote: 'Religion to Dawkins is like a red rag to a bull - evoking not merely an aggressive response, but one that throws normal scholarly conventions about scrupulous accuracy and fairness to the wind......Every one of Dawkins misrepresentations and overstatements can be challenged and corrected.....Dawkins clearly has little interest in engaging religious believers who will simply find themselves appalled by the flagrant misrepresentations of their beliefs and lifestyles....' In chapter 7, Dawkins asks, is the New Testament any better? He discounts the New Testament in 4 pages!

2. The Resurrection. We have, of course, already referred to the resurrection but many question the resurrection of Jesus. It is right when it is said that Christianity is based on the resurrection of Jesus

being a fact 'And, if Christ has not been raised, your faith is futile; you are still in your sins. '1 Cor. Ch 15 v 17. There is a great verse in Acts ch 26 v 8. Paul here is before King Agrippa, a Jew. 'If God has created the world and all things therein, why should any consider it incredible that God raises the dead?'

3. The Old Testament. I have been reading through the early books in the O.T. and I must confess that there are many things I do not understand. Judgment was severe - perhaps in those days it had to be. When we remember that Moses was dealing 'with a rabble of slaves' whom he had to shape into a nation - a Chosen People at that. But, the history of the Jews is absolutely remarkable. The Christian can trace the coming of Jesus right through the O.T. There is not time for us to look at that in detail but here are just two references from Isaiah, I'm sure familiar to all: 'For unto us a child is born, to us a son is given, and the government will be on His shoulders. And He will be called Wonderful, Counsellor, Mighty God, Everlasting Father.......' and 'He was oppressed and afflicted, yet He did not open His mouth; He was led like a lamb to the slaughter......' There are many many more prophecies which have been fulfilled. Richard Dawkins goes to great pains to criticise the O.T. He glories in the slaughter in this 'Christian book'. As mentioned, I find it hard to disagree with him! It seems that the O.T. displays a God of severe judgment while the N.T. reveals a God of Love. Are there then two Gods? The Gnostics of many years ago believed this. No, there are not two Gods. Jesus came to show us what God is like… Jesus did not have to change God's mind- God was love from the

beginning. What was lacking was man's understanding of God. So why did not God reveal Himself earlier? Paul writes to the Galatians: ' But when the time had fully come, God sent His Son.....' I am willing to leave God's timetable to Him.

4. The History of the Church. This is where things get difficult! The church cannot be proud of its history. Terrible things have been done in the name of the Christian religion - the Crusades, the persecution of the Jews, the fight between Roman Catholics and Protestants, we could add the times when individual Christians have brought shame on the name of Jesus - that includes you and me! On the TV a well-known atheist was cataloguing the faults of the church when Mervyn Bragg interrupted and said 'Hang on, what about the good things which the Christian Church has introduced into the world.' And, we could list all the blessings: the treatment of women and children., education, hospitals, health care. the abolishment of slavery (though it took a long time). We could think of what the church has tried and is trying to do throughout the world as an example. The church has a lot to answer for but there has been great progress amongst the churches for which we thank God and we trust that there will never be a time in the future when we will be ashamed of what the church does. For what it is worth, one journalist has written ' the destructive power of the secular religions, Marxism, Nazism, Maoism, far exceed the worst crimes of the Christian era.'. William Barclay writes: 'It is not too much to say that everything that has been done for the aged, the sick, the weak in body, and in mind, the

animal, the child, the woman has been done under the inspiration of Christianity.' Just look at history.

5. Following on from the previous point, we ought to consider the effect of the Christian faith on ordinary men, women, boys and girls. Millions, perhaps billions, have found forgiveness, peace, love, joy, power and purpose to live lives acceptable to God and themselves. We are told that the Christian Church is growing at a rate three times faster than the world population (according to a US Centre for World Mission). Consider the work of the Holy Spirit in your life. We know when we are at peace with Our Heavenly Father. In the U.K., it is true that the church is having a rough time, but there are many churches, where the work is fruitful and many people are finding God. It has to be said that the Christian life is demanding. Once a person finds Christ, there should follow a life of commitment. 'I no longer live but Christ lives in me' says Paul in Galatians ch 2. Maybe this is too much for some, but a life of fulfilment and joy follows.

6. What about Jesus? Although the church, its leaders and its members receive criticism, (often with justification) have you ever heard anyone criticise Jesus? Of course, His enemies who persuaded Pilate to crucify Him. They certainly did, but what about others? I remember Spike Milligan being asked whom he would like to invite for tea. He said 'Jesus'. On the basis of ethics alone, I think everyone would say they could not improve on the teachings of Jesus. Christianity turned world values upside down. The Sermon on the Mount - Matthew chs 5, 6 & 7:

'Blessed are the meek for they will inherit the earth.' 'If someone strikes you on the right cheek, turn to him the other also.' 'Love your enemies.' 'Do not worry about your life, what you will eat or drink...Is not life more important than food and the body more important than clothes? When Jesus was talking about John the Baptist - St Luke ch 7 v 28, He asked, What is this Kingdom, the first shall be last and the last first? And, when in St. John ch 13 v 2- 9 Jesus washed the feet of His disciples, what an example!

7. Creation and Revelation. We have thought much about spiritual revelation but what about natural revelation? Romans ch 1 v 18-23. Paul says: 'The wrath of God is being revealed against all the godlessness and wickedness of men who suppress the truth by their wickedness, since what may be known about God is plain to them. For since the creation of the world, God's invisible qualities..... have been clearly seen being understood from what has been made, so that men are without excuse.' Paul was disturbed by the number of idols in his day. In Athens, he said; 'Men of Athens! I see that in every way you are very religious, for as I walked around and looked carefully at your objects of worship, I even found an altar TO AN UNKNOWN GOD. Now what you worship as something unknown I am going to proclaim to you. The God who made the world and everything in it is the Lord of heaven and earth and does not live in temples made by human hands, as if He needed anything, because He Himself gives all men life and breath and everything else.....He is not far from each one of us. For in Him

we live and move and have our being.' This seems to be too simplistic but there are two beliefs: either the world just happened by chance and will end in utter chaos with no planned ending or the world was created by a loving God out of nothing and will end with an eternal plan of joy and praise, with no more suffering. In his book 'Why us' James Le Fanu writes: 'We might now, thanks to science, comprehend the universe of which we are part. only to discover that its properties as evolutionary biologist Richard Dawkins puts it, 'are precisely those we should expect if there is, at bottom, no design, no purpose, no evil and no good - nothing but blind, pitiless indifference'. Bertrand Russell also said, 'Brief and powerless is man's life, on his and all his race, the slow sure doom falls pitiless and dark.....' What an outlook! Many people, when considering the Heavens have declared 'It is so vast that I cannot believe the Creator is interested in me.' Don't let anyone rob you of the joy of knowing that God loves you, that you belong in His family. John writes: 'Jesus was in the world, and though, the world was made through Him, the world did not recognise Him.....Yet to all who received Him, to those who believed in His name, He gave the right to become children of God."

8. Just a short thought. I don't know about you, but would you not agree that a decision made in the context of eternity would be more reliable than one made on the basis of a short term?

9. The problem of suffering is one of the most challenging dilemmas for the Christian. No one

wants anyone to suffer except perhaps for a few who are completely lost in evil, corrupt and malicious motiveless practices which the rest of us cannot understand – even those are loved by Our Father God. We have freewill, a gift from the Lord and we need help to use it wisely. But what about this suffering problem. I am going to let the Rev. G.A. Studdert Kennedy (Woodbine Willie, a padre in W.W.1) answer for me. He wrote a poem called The Suffering God which has 19 verses and I am going to quote a little from the poem: ' How can it be that God can reign in glory, calmly content with what His love has done, Reading unmoved the piteous shameful story, All the vile deeds men do beneath the sun? Are there no tears in the heart of the Eternal? Is there no pain to pierce the soul of God? Then must He be a fiend of Hell infernal. Beating the earth to pieces with His rod. Father, if, He, the Christ, were Thy Revealer, Truly the First Begotten of the Lord, Then must Thou be a Suff'rer and a Healer, Pierced to the heart by the sorrow of the sword.' If you have the opportunity to read the whole of this poem, please do so. God is present in all our sufferings. When someone dies, it is those who are left who suffer and the Lord is with them. Those who die find comfort with the Lord. I am always amazed when someone visits a children's ward in a hospital, again and again, those who are ill seem to shine with a wonderful strength and peace. Kasoh Kitamori argued that true love was rooted in pain. God's own pain and suffering enables Him to give meaning and dignity to the human experience and heals our pain. Can you imagine a world without

19

pain, no fellow feeling, no reason to care for anyone else?

10. In all seriousness, how can the problems of this world be solved? Can we find the answer in politics, education, capitalism, democracy, evolution, materialism, astrology, philosophy, communism, humanism? Other religions? No other religion makes the claims of the Christian faith, because no other religion has Jesus Christ. You will never guess where I found the following words. Let me quote them to you: 'Everybody has to have some criteria on which to base their personal morality, so from where are these criteria derived...? In fact, the personal morality of most seems to stem from the corrupt, commercial and venal values of the market economy - - instant gratification, greed, selfishness and self-interest, hype, spin, materialism and the primacy of consumption in preference to the life of the mind. The only result of that is individual misery, social mayhem and planetary destruction.......We live in a society founded on deceit, duplicity and deception in which hypocrisy and mendacity are endemic.' (Edward Greengold B.A., A.C.I.B.) These words were found in a banker's journal! The only regret I have is that the words did not give us the solution to the problems set out. So much suffering these days seems to be self-inflicted. I believe with all my heart that the answer for me and you, the town in which we live, our nation, the whole world is faith and trust in the Lord Jesus Christ. I believe that His claims on our lives are twofold. First. He made us and then He bought us by His precious blood. So, in what do you believe? G.K. Chesterton said that a

man who does not believe in God will believe in
something worse. I say, that I cannot believe in
anything better!

Chapter 2
God's Promises

l guess we all make promises from time to time. The trouble is, it is easy to make them but sometimes very difficult to keep them: 'Do you have in your treasure of memories some instance of a promise made but not fulfilled? Thomas Fuller, 17th century churchman, said: 'Apt to promise is apt to forget. 'I think he could be right but another of his quotes was: 'We are born crying, live complaining and die disappointed.' I don't like that one! Back to promises, I expect we have all failed someone by a broken promise. Dear Lord forgive us.

Politicians make promises! Politicians of every flavour. We wouldn't mind so much if they owned up to it but often the promises are so vague that they get away with it.

What about advertisements? Even if the advertisers are criticized they still carry on advertising, and we are duped again and again. Who remembers the promise boxes? When I was a lad, it was customary to take a promise from the box – a promise being a verse of Scripture.

There is a book edited by Herbert Lockyer called 'All the promises of the Bible'. Promises you can stand on through thick and thin. In this book there are over 8000 promises - not only that but thousands of them have been fulfilled, the rest have yet to be fulfilled. ·

Dwight L. Moody said, 'Take the promise of God. Let a man feed for a month on the promises of God, and he will not talk about how poor he is......If you would only read from Genesis to Revelation and see all the promises made by God to Abraham....and to all the Gentiles, and to all His people everywhere......you would lift up your head and proclaim the riches of His Grace, because you couldn't help doing it.'

Here are just a few of those promises relating to Jesus and they have all been fulfilled. God does not make idle promises. His promises are sure.

The first promise about Jesus was in Genesis ch 3 v 15 when God spoke to the serpent in the Garden of Eden: 'And I will put enmity between you and the woman, and between your offspring and hers; he will crush your head and you will strike his heel.' Performance: Galatians ch. 4 v 4: 'But when the time had fully come, God sent His Son, born of a woman. Born under law, to redeem those under the law, that we might receive the full rights of sons.'

To Abraham, Genesis ch 17 v 7: I will establish my covenant as an everlasting covenant between me and you and your descendants after you.... Performance: Galatians ch 3 v 16: 'The promises were spoken to Abraham and to his seed....'

To David, Psalm 132 v 11: 'The Lord swore an oath to David... .' Performance: Matthew ch 1 v I: Jesus Christ. the Son of David... '

To Mary, Isaiah ch 7 v 14: 'The virgin will be with child and will give birth to a Son, and will call Him Immanuel.' Performance: Matthew ch l v 18: 'His mother Mary was pledged to Joseph, but before they came together, she was found to be with child through the Holy Spirit.

His birth, Micah ch 5 v 2: 'But you Bethlehem Ephrathah though you are small among the clans of Judah, out of you will come for me one who will be ruler over Israel. Performance: Matthew ch 2 v I: 'After Jesus was born in Bethlehem... '

To John the Baptist, Malachi ch 3 v I: 'See, I will send my messenger, who will prepare the way before Me.' Performance: Matthew ch 3 v 1: 'In those days, John the Baptist came...

There are many, many more promises relating to Jesus' rejection, betrayal, sale for 30 pieces and suffering., e.g. Psalm 22 v 16: 'they have pierced my hands and my feet.' Performance: John ch 19 v 18: 'Here they crucified Him...' His burial Isaiah ch 53 v 9: 'He was assigned a grave with the wicked and with the rich in His death. Performance· Matthew ch 27 v 59: 'Joseph took the body, wrapped it in a clean cloth, and placed it in his own new tomb.' And finally, the resurrection Psalm 16 v 10: 'Because, You will not abandon Me to the grave.' Performance: Luke ch 24 v 6: He is not here; He has risen!' Hallelujah!! Now, at God's right hand, Psalm 110 v I: 'The Lord says to my Lord: Sit at my right hand.' Performance: Hebrews ch 1 v 3: 'He sat down at the right hand of the Majesty in Heaven.

A SUMMARY OF GOD'S PROMISES ABOUT JESUS

PROMISES	FULFILLED
1.As the seed of the woman: Genesis 3 v 15	Galatians 4 v 4: But when the time had fully come, God sent His Son, born of a woman, born under the law, that we might receive the full rights of sons.
2.His being born of a virgin: Isaiah 7 v 14	Luke2 v 7 and she gave birth to her firstborn, a son.....
3.Bom in Bethlehem Micah 5 v 2	Matthew 2 v 1 After Jesus was born in Bethlehem.....
4.Slaying of children Jeremiah 31 v 15	Matthew 2 v 16 Herod was furious and he gave orders to kill all the boys.....
5.Anointed with the Spirit: God has set You above your companions by anointing You Psalm 45 v 7	Matthew 3 v 16 As soon as Jesus was baptized, He saw the Spirit of God descending like a dove....

6.He will honour Galilee Isaiah 9 v 1	Matthew 4 v 12 He returned to Galilee
7.Speaking in parables. Psalm 78 v 2 I will open my mouth in parables	Matthew 13 v 34 He did not say anything without using a parable
8. Miracles- then will the eyes of the blind be opened...... Isaiah 35 v 5,6	John 11 v 47 Here is this man performing miraculous signs....
9.Rejection Psalm 118 v 22	John 7 v 48 Has any of the rulers or of the Pharisees believed in Him?
10.Betrayed Psalm 41 v 9 Even my close friend…	John 13 v 18 He who shares bread has lifted up his heel...
11.Suffering: all chapter Isaiah 53	Matthew 20 v 28 To give His life
12.Scourged Isaiah 10 v 6 I offered my back to those who beat me...	Mark 14 v 65 they blindfolded Him struck Him with their fists....
13.Forsaken: My God why have you forsaken me Psalm 22 v 1	Matthew 27 v 46 My God, why have you forsaken me...

teaching. My Father will love him and we will come to him and make our home with him.

John ch 16 v 33:....In this world you will have trouble. But take heart! I have overcome the world.

Read *Acts* ch 2 v 14 - 21 where Peter repeats what the prophet Joel predicted in his book ch 2 v 28-32-the pouring out of the Holy Spirit on all flesh.

Romans ch 8 v 28: And we .know that in all things God works for the good of those who love Him who have been called according to His purpose.

Romans ch 8 v 32: He did not spare His own Son, but gave Him up for us all...…

I Corinthians ch 15 v 57: But thanks be to God! He gives us the victory through our Lord Jesus Christ.

2 Corinthians ch 12 v 9: My grace is sufficient for you, for my power is made perfect in weakness.

Galatians ch 4 v 28: Now you, brothers like Isaac, are children of promise.

Galatians ch 6 v 9: Let us not become weary in doing good, for at the proper time we will reap a harvest if we do not give up.

Read Philippians ch 4 v 4-7 and v 13: I can do everything through Him who gives me strength and v 19: And my God will meet all your needs according to His glorious riches in Christ Jesus.

Hebrews ch 2 v 18: Because He Himself suffered when He was tempted, he is able to help those who are being tempted.

Read Hebrews ch 4 v 14-16.

Hebrews ch 7 v 24,25: But because Jesus lives for ever, He has a **permanent** priesthood. Therefore, He is able to save completely those who come to God through Him. because He always lives to intercede for them.

I hope. like me. you have been overcome by the wealth of these promises. And, these are just a few of the hundreds in God's Word. And, finally:

Matthew 28 v 19,20: 'Therefore go and make disciples of all nations, baptising them in the name of the Father and of the Son and of the Holy Spirit, teaching them to obey everything I have commanded you. And surely I am with you always, to the very end of the age.' David Livingstone's favourite verse. He said. 'That's the word of a perfect gentleman and that's the end of it.'

Chapter 3
Revelation

How do we learn things? They are revealed to us. What is my name? How do you know? What do you know about me? How many ears have I? How many toes? *As* most people have ten toes, it seems fairly safe to assume that I also have ten toes.

Can I ask you to use your imagination? Let's imagine that we had been born in a house without windows and that we had lived there quite happily - eating, drinking, playing, learning, exercising (we hadn't known anything different) then one day, the door was opened and for the first time we saw a beautiful garden.

What would be our reaction? We would touch the grass, examine the flowers - wonder and amazement would be shown in our faces. Then in the distance, we could see fields, trees, rivers, mountains. As the light gradually faded, the stars would pop into view. We would probably find it difficult to take it all in.

But, of course, we do have access to all these wonders. And, no doubt, we still need words to express our feelings. Psalm 8, 19, 24 – Psalm 14!

What does the world around us reveal? Two friends, a Christian and an atheist, were walking around an airfield. The Christian pointed to an aircraft and said, 'Look at the aircraft, how do you think it was created?' The atheist replied, 'Well of course, it was created in a factory.' 'No,' said the Christian, 'there was a heap of junk metal and the bits joined themselves to produce an aircraft.' 'Now, that is ridiculous,' the atheist answered. 'But, my friend, that is how you want me to believe the world was created!'

There has, it seems, always been a confrontation between the creationists and the evolutionists. A high school is teaching the creationist theory which is being attacked by the evolutionists. I think they are both off the truth. I believe God created the universe. I do not know if God created it in six days though Peter says that a 1000 years is like a day to God. Some of Charles Darwin's writings were referring to the laws of creation a few mornings ago. If God had wanted to use evolution, then who am I to criticize. I repeat, I believe God created the universe. What is the alternative? It made itself!

Acts ch 17 v 22-28. This is how Paul saw things and he tried to explain his faith to the learned men of Athens. The evidence around us is called 'natural revelation' and Paul maintains that it says a lot about God.

Romans ch I v 18-23. Throughout Paul's life he had been dying to get to Rome. He wanted to preach the Gospel of the Lord Jesus to the centre of the Roman Empire but he also knew what a disappointment Rome would be. Rome had been described as a 'cesspool of iniquity' 'a filthy sewer' - it was a city full of idols and behaviour to match. He tried to appeal to the natural things they could see around them. 'God has made it plain' he says. Indeed, says Paul, in the next chapter of Romans, God has also written a law on your hearts, ch 2 v 14-16.

Where do we think this law on our hearts has come from?

There is then natural revelation around us and within us. These sources should make us think about the One behind all creation.

Another source of revelation is seen in the history of the Jews- God's Chosen people, but maybe this is not a source we want to examine too much at this moment with all the conflict and suffering that is taking place. We certainly need to pray for peace.

But, a verse from Hebrews ch 1 v 1,2 shows how God finally revealed Himself to us in Jesus, God's Supreme revelation to man. We see in Jesus what God is really like: love, forgiveness, grace, power, victory over sin and death.

Romans ch 8 v 1-4 and 37-39. I guess the next part of this article is to ask what you are going to do with all this revelation - the wonderful world in which we live, our consciences, the world's history and finally God's revelation in Jesus Christ, Our Lord and Saviour, because it all demands a response.

Have you heard the phrase 'the claims of Christ'? From this revelation we can see that Jesus has two claims, as has already been said, on our lives. (i) He made us and (ii) He bought us.

Chapter 4
Some Christian History

Christianity was born geographically where east meets west in the centre of the then known world. It was born spiritually between the Jews and the Gentiles, between religions legalism and the pursuit of Greek philosophy.

Galilee though was comfortably removed from the more strict Judaism of Jerusalem. It is believed that only Judas, out of all the disciples. was from Judea. There was from the start a greater adaptability to Gentile ways. However, Jesus encountered the strictness of Judaism in His meeting with the Pharisees and the teachers of the Law. St Matthew ch 23 contains great condemnation of these people who had built out of the law inhuman restrictions on normal behaviour. In His dealings with the materialistic Sadducees who only accepted the first five books of the Old Testament, He showed that they were not aware of the message which they contained. St Matthew ch 22 v 29 'You are in error because you do not know the Scriptures or the power of God'.

The Herodians were a political party. They accepted the rule of Rome and were obsequious for their own ends. Their main opponents were the Zealots who would only acknowledge Jehovah as King.

It is believed that the Essenes originated during the time of the Maccabees under a teacher of Righteousness. They were a tightly controlled group who had withdrawn into communities and who were seeking a true understanding of the Law. It was believed that only the men possessed this understanding and were referred to as the Sons of light.

When the early church was scattered after Pentecost and particularly with the conversion of Paul, the early Christians were introduced to Greek philosophies. We have in Paul's trip to Athens a wonderful insight into some of these philosophies and also an insight into Paul's learning. We meet with the Epicureans and Stoics Paul uses quotations in his message from Epimenides and Aratus of Cilicia.

Christianity arrived early in Rome, the capital of the Empire. We do not know how! (This is a great challenge as well as consolation, for the Word spread by travelling converts—as in the early days of the Salvation Army. What would I do in my town if I was the only Christian?).

The Roman authorities were obviously faced with a new phenomenon and early on were not sure how to understand it or its relationship with Judaism.

It seems possible that Peter visited Rome before Paul, who having appealed with Caesar (Acts ch 25 v 11) was sent to the city for trial. As often with a new group, the Christians attracted suspicion and hostility from both Jews and pagans. Claudius had had trouble in AD 51 and Nero in AD 64 blamed the disastrous fire in Rome on the Christians. It is believed that both Peter and Paul were martyred around this time.

After the fire, it is not certain what attitude the authorities had to the Christians. It is not believed that

14.Garments Psalm 22 v 18 They divide my garments among them and casts lots for my clothing...	Matthew 27 35 they divided up His clothes by casting lots....
15.Resurrection Psalm 16 v 9-11	Luke24 v 6 He is not here, He is risen

Even More promises for us for today:

Psalm 23 v 1: The Lord is my Shepherd. I shall not want.....

Psalm 34 v 10: The lions may grow weak and hungry, but those who seek the Lord lack no good thing.

We have all the countless promises of the Old Testament, plus those of the New Testament. It is possible to record just a few from the New. No doubt, you have your own favourites but here is a small selection:

Matthew ch 7 v 7: Ask and it will be given to you; seek and you will find; knock and the door will be opened to you.

Matthew ch 28 v 20:......And surely, I am with you always, to the very end of the age.

John ch 14 v 16 and 23: And I will ask the Father, and He will give you another Counsellor to be with you for ever. Jesus replied, 'If anyone loves Me, he will obey my they were outlawed, but they were still treated with great suspicion. Tacitus, the Roman historian, describes Christians as 'enemies of the human race'. It would appear that if there was any reason to arrest Christians, they would only be able to clear themselves by offering a sacrifice to the Emperor, an act that the faithful would not accept with due outcome.

Roman attitudes to religion were a great disappointment to Paul. Rome was described as a 'sewer of iniquity' and it seemed that the Romans used any excuse to pursue any doubtful pleasure. The Roman Emperors adopted different attitudes to divinity from Julius Caesar and Caligula who assumed divinity to the 'rough old soldier' Vespasian who when dying jokingly remarked 'I think I am becoming a god'.

J. W. C. Wand sums up the opening of the Christian era thus 'Judaism contributed to the best culture of the time monotheism and morality, Rome organization, Greece philosophy, the East mysticism and a gift for worship. Of all these Christianity was to take advantage'.

Chapter 5
Titles of the Deity

Now in my eighties, I feel I am becoming a grumpy old man! The cause of my present grumpiness is the way Our Lord and Saviour is referred to when using pronouns i.e. he and not He. I must confess that I find this annoying. To be honest, I did not notice this practice in the A.V. but, having used the N.I.V. (which I love) for some years it still causes a little bother.

After a little research, I am somewhat more content. Biblica, publisher of the N.I.V. says: The N.I.V. and some other contemporary translations do not capitalise these pronouns for a very good reason: they are not capitalised in the original. The Greek does not use upper case in employing these pronouns and Hebrew uses only capital letters and has no lower case letters. Also, it says: the decision to capitalise or not to capitalise is a question of translation and is not a statement of disrespect.

This is certainly acceptable with regard to translations of scripture, but what about our song/hymn books. There does not appear to be any reason why lower case pronouns should be used in our song books. When I write 'My wife and I. ..' no one would accept 'My wife and i'. Why do I receive a capital pronoun and my Lord does not?

From Bible Gateway (U.S. -Andy Rau):

'Some Bibles do not capitalise certain pronouns because their translators felt that doing so was not an accurate translation of the original language. The decision to capitalise or not to capitalise pronouns is a question of translation and is not a statement of disrespect. For example, here is a note from a translation consultant for the NIV addressing this question:

> The NIV and some other contemporary translations do not capitalise these pronouns for a very good reason: they are not capitalised in the original. The Greek does not use upper case in employing these pronouns and Hebrew uses only capital letters and has no lowercase letters.
>
> The translators had to face a difficult issue and thought about it long and hard. On the one hand was the practice of showing reverence to God in keeping with the common English usage and on the other hand was their commitment to provide a precise rendering of the original with no bowing to what was not in the original text. In the end they decided that fidelity to the original was their highest criterion.
>
> While we may not like the absence of the uppercase letters, we can respect their total commitment to their precise rendering of the original.
>
> – Biblica, Publisher of the NIV

Chapter 6
Faith (Hebrews ch 11 v 1–10)

There are a few different senses in which we use this word. Although in every day conversation we don't use the word a great deal. We may talk about having faith in a person. We would probably say 'we trust so and so'. We don't normally say we have faith in things. But, I have a Skoda car and so I may well say I have faith in my car!!

This morning we got up, we didn't question whether the floor would hold us up. We went into the bathroom and didn't question the quality of the water, maybe we did think about those poor people who have been flooded and for whom it is not a normal day surrounded by water of a questionable quality. We may even have thought about those people for whom a normal day is walking a fair distance to collect water for the day. Back to our kitchens - we collected some cereal and reached for the milk. Did you smell the milk before pouring it on the cereal? Some people have a habit of doing that. I think there was a TV programme where someone always smelt the milk. Perhaps they had had an unfortunate experience with the milk some time ago. Anyway, we had breakfast, washed, bathed or showered, shaved, dressed, left home for the church and here we are. We entered the church and sat down. We have exercised a great deal of faith in various things to get to this position.

During the preparation of this article, there was a TV news item about airline pilots falling asleep. One Captain asked the First Officer to take over while he had a rest. Later, he looked over to see the First Officer also asleep and the aircraft was turning into the path of another plane. Apparently airline pilots are being asked to fly more and more hours.........

What happens when someone or something lets us down? It is not the faith that has failed it is the thing or person in whom we placed our trust. We have all been let down by someone and I'm sure we have all let someone down. We have betrayed their trust and that is a terrible thing and we have been so sorry. We have all been let down by things, washing machines, cars, alarms, you name it. ...

So we all know that definition of faith or trust, when someone or thing, which we trusted has let us down. Many of us here know the positive side of faith and trust. We know Someone who will never let us down. Indeed, we can safely say that the Lord Jesus is without doubt the only One in whom we can place our faith knowing that our faith will be safe and rewarded.

In the Bible we read (Romans ch 4 v 3) 'Abraham believed God and it was credited to him as righteousness.' This is not easy to understand. Abraham trusted God and because he fully and completely gave his life to God and was obedient to Him, he became right with God. The Jews also found this difficult to understand because years later, they insisted on an obedience to the Law. William Barclay says, 'The basic thought of the Jews was that a man must earn God's favour "by keeping the Law". The basic thought of Christianity is that a man can never earn God's favour, that all he can do is to take God at His word and stake everything on the faith that God's promises are true.'

Wm Barclay again 'It is the supreme discovery of the Christian life that we do not need to torture ourselves with a losing battle to earn God's love, all we need to do is to accept in perfect trust the love which God offers to us. True, after that any man of honour is under the life-long obligation to seek to be worthy of that love. But he is no longer a criminal seeking to obey an impossible law; he is a lover offering his all to One who loved him when he never deserved it.'

Some Christians still believe that we have to earn Heaven. We cannot and will never be able to earn Heaven. It is a gift of God's love. All we have to do is to love God in return with all our heart, mind and strength.

Another meaning of faith is The Faith - the Christian Religion. Faith has also been described as an unshakeable belief in something especially without proof. There are some people who have no faith whatsoever in religions of any sort and there are those who think that there is no evidence for the Christian faith. I am sorry but I do have to mention again Richard Dawkins, who has written a book 'The God Delusion'. He is a scientist who has become an evangelical fundamental atheist On page 5, he writes: 'If this book works as I intend, religious readers who open it will be atheists when they put it down.'

So faith in the Christian Faith is indeed a step in the dark, but it is not blind faith. There is ample evidence in the fact that millions have found forgiveness, peace, power, purpose, fulfilment, joy...........

We have thought about the meaning of the word 'faith' and we have considered the Christian Faith, putting the two together we come to another meaning of complete and absolute trust in a person, the Lord Jesus Christ The initial step of faith develops into a 'blessed assurance' and comforting knowledge of the Lord Jesus who lives within our hearts, guides us, empowers us, fills us with a deep sense of joy and peace. Then we can say with Paul: 'I know whom I have believed and am convinced that He is able to guard what I have entrusted to Him for that day'. Jesus is the only answer to life's problems. But, we haven't finished yet. There's still another meaning of faith to consider. It also means loyalty, our faithfulness to the cause. We started thinking about trust in people and things. Has Jesus got our faith and trust. We have to confess that we have let Him down so many times. Let us be determined to be faithful, to ask Him what He wants of us and then to obey.

Chapter 7
Plans

On a Thursday morning selling the War Crys (Salvation Army paper), I see all kinds of people moving around. Some have a definite purpose and know exactly where they are going. Others seem a bit aimless, hesitant, going hither and thither and then I see them again. The difference, of course, is that the purposeful group have a list, a plan, while the others are relying on their memories which let them down. Plans are essential for a smooth operation. We are making plans most of the time. Holiday plans, some rely on Holiday companies, some do it all themselves. Finance plans, or do you find too much month over at the end of the money?

If we are in business and in need of cash. the bank will demand a Cash Budget and forecast final accounts in order to see if we can repay the loan, which is after all the banks money. Governments need plans for the country but we seem to hear about u-tums all the time.

Plans are essential but at the same time, no one knows what tomorrow will bring. No one knows what will happen tomorrow. We are in a cleft stick. No matter what we do, the future is uncertain. So, we come up with plan 'B' or we need to call Baldrick of Blackadder to see if he has a cunning plan!

1. Some believe that there is no plan for our world. G. N. Clark said, 'There is no secret and no plan in history to be discovered. I do not believe that any future consummation could make sense of all the irrationalities of preceding ages.' Andre Maurois said, 'The universe is

indifferent. Who created it? Why are we here on the puny mud-heap spinning in infinite space? I have not the slightest idea and I am quite convinced that no one has the least idea' Bertrand Russell,' Brief and powerless is man's life, on his and all his race, the slow sure doom falls pitiless and dark...' What an outlook! Scientific atheists seem to be expressing their opinions more strongly than they used to.

2. But there is a plan. William Barclay writes: 'It is the conviction that history is a plan that history has a purpose that history is the working out of the will of God. Ephesians ch 1 v 5-10. A secret or a mystery was given to Paul, which is now given to all of us. A secret which was a purpose or plan which was formed before the world began. History is being controlled until it reaches its full development when all things in Heaven and earth are gathered into one in Jesus. Now this sounds rather complicated but what it means is that the gospel was open not just for Jews but for the Gentiles; for all people everywhere.

Atheists know something of the truth because, we all know the state of the world, a world which was left to mankind. It is indeed in a terrible state. We think of wars and strife. We think of Syria We think of individual people who have a civil war operating in their lives. 'Jesus came to make the world into one world in Himself.'

3. So there is a plan for the world. What then is this plan? Listen to these verses: 'For God has bound all men over to disobedience so that He may have mercy on them all.' Roman ch 5 v 18. 'For as in Adam all die, so in Christ all will be made alive.' 1 Corinthians ch 15 v 22. 'that at the

name of Jesus every knee should bow, in Heaven and on earth and under the earth and every tongue confess that Jesus Christ is Lord to the Glory of God the Father' Philippians ch 2 v 10,11. 'The Lord is not slow in keeping His promise, as some understand slowness. He is patient with you, not wanting anyone to perish, but everyone to come to repentance. 2 Peter ch 3 v 9. 'For here we do not have an enduring city, but we are looking for the city which is to come.' Hebrews ch 13 v 14. And in the meantime, there is a plan for every man, woman, boy and girl. There is a plan for you, no matter how old, young, fit, active, inactive. We can all pray and prayer makes a difference. Pray for that person who you find it difficult to speak to. Pray for the sick, pray for your neighbours. ...Dear Lord, help us all to cooperate in your plan, help us faithfully to do our part. Amen.

Chapter 8
Gnosticism

How did Gnosticism endanger Christian thinking?

Gnosticism 'by derivation – it implies the 'pursuit of esoteric knowledge' or the pursuit of knowledge that is only intended for the enlightened few. It is unfortunate that most men seem to pursue membership of the elite – whatever that may mean!

It is difficult to arrive at a simple explanation of Gnosticism as there were many forms of it but basically it was a philosophy that was dualist. Its followers saw a materialistic universe that was evil and a spiritual universe that was good.

One theologian (Marcion) influenced by Gnostic ideas maintained that there were two Gods - the God of the Old Testament (evil) and the God of the New Testament (good). The earliest gnostic was possibly Simon Magus (Acts ch. 8) who put great store on the magical arts. Saturninus taught salvation by asceticism. Basilides had 365 heavens and Valentius maintained that the fullness of the Godhead involved 30 aeons and that there were three classes of men. Jesus was often included as a Messiah but only as a representative of God and certainly not human.

The dangers of Gnosticism were that it was more concerned with enlightenment than morality, it sought escape from matter rather than from sin and its aims were philosophical rather than religious. It was certainly not Scriptural. It is not surprising that Gnostics eventually began to form sects outside the church. It is incredible that these strange ideas took hold but then there are always some people who will adopt the craziest of ideas.

However, there is always a silver lining for these movements challenged the church which established a threefold defence: (i) a canon of Scripture (ii) the episcopate – the bishops who would safeguard the tradition and truth of the church and (iii) the creed of Christian doctrine establishing the truth of the Gospel in straightforward language. There was also much Christian literature to combat the heretical literature that abounded.

Chapter 9
Joseph

Joseph had ten older brothers, so we could be led to believe that he was spoilt by them. Unfortunately, this was far from the truth. His ten older brothers had the same father but different mothers.

Joseph's father was Jacob who as a young man fell in love with a beautiful young lady named Rachel. Jacob was desperate to marry Rachel so he approached her father Laban and suggested that he worked for seven years in return for Rachel. This was agreed, but Laban was not a man of his word. Jacob set his heart on working hard for his love for seven years, which seemed to him just a few days. Laban was a greedy man and he deceived Jacob giving him his elder daughter, Leah, by trickery. Jacob did eventually win Rachel by working another seven years!

So, we have Jacob with two wives. Leah gave Jacob four sons. Poor Rachel gave him none creating a difficult situation and experiencing the disgrace which accompanied barrenness in those days. Rachel thought it might help if she gave her maidservant, Bilboa, to Jacob again in accordance with the custom to produce a son by proxy. Bilboa gave Jacob two more sons. Leah had stopped having children, so she gave Jacob her maidservant, Zilpah who produced two more sons.

The Bible says that God remembered Rachel who became pregnant and gave birth to Joseph but later she died giving birth to Benjamin. Jacob ended up with twelve sons: Leah - 6, Bilboa- 2, Zilpah- 2, Rachel -2.

There were times when Joseph told tales to his father about his brothers and as the favourite (Rachel's son) Jacob gave to Joseph a richly ornamented robe. In addition to all this Joseph started having dreams in which his brothers bowed down to Joseph as sheaves in one dream and stars in another - and Joseph told this to his brothers! Joseph's popularity reached hidden depths.

Joseph's life hadn't started very well, but it got even worse. A summary follows: 1. He was all but murdered by his brothers when he took them some sustenance. 2. He was put into a pit, hopefully, to perish. 3. He was sold to Ishmaelites traders. 4. He was sold as a slave. 5. After making good progress and prospering in his Master's house, he was thrown into prison for allegedly making advances to his Master's wife. Joseph was innocent. 6. During his time in prison, he interprets two dreams correctly one for the chief cupbearer (who was punished) and another for the butler. 7. Two years pass, Joseph is still in prison, and the Pharaoh has a couple of dreams. The chief cupbearer, in prison, is reminded of Joseph's skill in interpreting dreams which he passes on to the Pharaoh.

Joseph is summoned and he interprets the dreams for the Pharaoh. This results in Joseph being elevated to a very high position with the responsibility of dealing with seven years of abundance followed by seven years of famine. Joseph exercises great efficiency so that when the famine starts Egypt is in good shape to cope, so much so that surrounding countries look to Egypt for help. Jacob and his family are amongst those in need of grain and they set off to Egypt with the exception of Benjamin who has become the favourite.

On arrival in Egypt, they are recognised by Joseph. However, Joseph with his Egyptian dress and position of Governor remains unrecognised, but he deals with the brothers harshly. He calls them spies. They are quick to explain their position and tell Joseph about their father, family and young brother. Eventually, Joseph allows them to return home on condition that they bring the young brother next time. Joseph demands a hostage and Simeon has to stay behind. Joseph also orders their payment of silver to be put into their sacks. Jacob is furious on their return home. Why was the silver still in their sacks? Why tell the Egyptian Governor about Benjamin? What is going to happen to Simeon? Jacob was determined that Benjamin would not go to Egypt, but the food ran out! They had to return with double the silver. Nothing else must go wrong.

Joseph felt he had to reveal himself on their return and later there was a great reunion with Jacob too. After a happy time, Jacob died, but now the brothers were anxious. What would Joseph do, get his own back? Joseph said, 'Don't be afraid. Am I in place of God? You intended to harm me but God intended it for good to accomplish what is now being done, the saving of many lives.....and he reassured them.'

Romans ch 8 v 28 'And we know that in all things God works for the good of those who love Him, who have been called according to His purpose.'

Chapter 10
Worry

Philippians ch 4 v 6 (reading 4-9)

My mother was a worrier. If there was nothing to worry about she would worry! Do you worry?

Two old chaps talking: Joe: You look downhearted, old man, what are you worried about? Bill: The future. Joe: What makes your future look so hopeless? Bill: My past!

1. Do you worry about the past? Listen to this quote:

It is the opening of Aldous Huxley's – the writer and humanist – 'Brave New World':

'Chronic remorse, as all the moralists are agreed, is a most undesirable sentiment. If you have behaved badly, repent, make what amends you can and address yourself to the task of behaving better next time. On no account brood over your wrongdoing. Rolling in the muck is not the best way of getting clean.'

Now, we Christians have absolutely no need to worry about the past. Here are some verses: Psalm 103 v 11,12, Romans ch 8 v 1-4 and Psalm 51 v 10-12. We have all done things of which we are ashamed. I know I have. But I trust like David, we have all asked Jesus to forgive and cleanse our hearts.

If you haven't..........Praise God the above applies also to you.

2. The Present. Do you worry about the present? St Matthew ch 6 v 25-34. Eating, drinking, clothes (the row

about school uniform), money - we have to be sensible. Do we feel we have to make a good impression by what we wear? When Diane and I going out, she changes her dress a few times. I say to Diane, 'Don't worry.' She will say, 'I'm not worried, but someone has to care.' Now I find this a bit difficult. If we do not worry, it does not mean we do not care. It means we take it to the Lord. William Barclay says, we must remember three things: (1) We must remember the Love of God and His love is for all people. (2) We must remember the Wisdom of God. He knows what is best for us all. And (3) We must remember the Power of God. He can bring to pass that which is best for us.

When we hear about the terrible things which are happening in the Middle East, all we can do is to pray, but James ch 2 v 14-17....If we truly care and there is something that we can do, we should do it.

3. The Future. Anxiety is to have no place in the life of a Christian because for everything there is prayer. Bengel said, 'Anxiety and prayer are more opposed to each other than fire and water.' Thanksgiving should always accompany prayer because it is always due to God, and after prayer and thanksgiving, there is peace.

Alec Motyer: 'The antidote to anxiety, and the prelude to the enjoyment of peace, are to be found in the linked exercise of prayer and thanksgiving. In prayer, anxiety is resolved by trust in God. That which causes the anxiety is brought to the One who is totally competent and in whose hands the matter can be left.'

Chapter 11
Gold

Throughout human history man has been infatuated by and has searched for gold. There are countless stories and films about men looking for gold and gold rushes. What is it about gold that tempts men to take all kinds of risks to acquire it? Have you got hoards of gold? Gold teeth? Gold watches? Gold jewellery? Gold rings?

(i) It is beautiful, attractive. It has been used to create some of the world's most treasured works of art and beautiful jewellery.

(ii) Compared to most things it is durable and does not tarnish or corrode, it retains its beauty. We have a collection of about 90 brass bells, the front door a brass letterbox, knocker and handle!! Now, if they were gold....

(iii) Another quality which helps in its attraction is that gold is soft and malleable. Although it is one of the heaviest of metals, it is malleable, in other words it can be worked on, hammered or shaped without breaking. If I had an ounce of gold, something like 4 x 50p (English 50p coins) it could be beaten out to 187sq ft, roughly a 13.5 ft square - we would call that gold leaf. Many of the buildings in the middle east are covered with gold leaf. In Exodus ch 39, we read about the priestly garments. 'They made the ephod of gold.....they hammered out thin sheets of gold and cut strands to be worked into blue, purple and scarlet yarn and fine linen'

(iv) Gold is ductile, it can be stretched like chewing gum! In theory an ounce of gold can be stretched many miles to as thin as 0.0004 inches.

(v) Gold is a good conductor of heat and electricity and is used in electronics. Its qualities are valuable in dentistry and also more recently in space research in satellites and space suits and because of its reflection qualities in windows of large office buildings.

(vi) Gold is scarce. And therefore has been used as a medium of exchange for centuries - gold bullion, coins, even notes! In 1981, the government of Antigua and Barbuda issued gold notes to mark their independence. Gold between nations is still a reserve asset, about 45% of the world's gold is held by governments.

Where does it come from? It is difficult to see and find It's not found in convenient chunks but is found with copper and lead deposits and is invisible to the human eye. Sometimes larger flakes can be found. Where? California, Australia, Egypt, Turkey, Iran, India, China, S. Africa, Russia, S. America and Wales! The Romans operated gold mines in Wales. The first official discovery was in 1843. The Dolgellau gold belt in N. Wales has produced about 4 tons of gold. Today, it is described as a cottage industry run by local people.

The main producers today are S. Africa, Russia, Australia and the U.S.A. The Smithsonian Institute in the U.S.A. maintains that there are 45 trillion dollars' worth of gold in the ocean.

(vii) Gold is soft and often has to be mixed with other metals for jewellery and coins - silver, copper, nickel or zinc. Gold content is expressed in karats. 24K is pure gold, 12K is 50% gold.

(viii) Gold is a royal metal. What incident in the Bible shows us that?

Peter did not have a great respect for gold or should I say he had a healthy respect for the metal. 1 Peter ch 1 v 7 'your faith – of greater worth than gold, which perishes even though refined by fire - may be proved genuine...' 1 Peter ch 1 v 18 'For you know that it was not with perishable things such *as* gold or silver that you were redeemed from the empty way of life....but by the precious blood of Christ.' 1 Peter ch 3 v 3 'Your beauty should not come from outward adornment, such *as* braided hair and the wearing of gold jewellery and fine clothes. Instead, it should come from your inner self, the unfading beauty of a gentle and quiet spirit... ' Do you remember when Peter and John found a crippled man, he said, ' Silver and gold I do not have, but what I have I give you. In the name of Jesus Christ of Nazareth. walk!'

However, I think Peter will forgive me if I say that there are many things we can learn from gold and its qualities. We are told to be *as* good *as* gold!

We should be:

(i) Beautiful! Let the beauty of Jesus be seen in me.

(ii) Durable. Gold stays bright. Are we temperamental, moody? 'He who stands firm to the end will be saved' Mark ch 13 v 13.

(iii) Malleable, ductile adaptable. Paul said, 'I have become all things to all men so that by all possible means I might save some.' 1 Corinthians ch 9 v 22.

(iv) Soft. Tender-hearted, kind.

(v) Good conductor. A means of helping things along. We are not barriers that others have to climb over. We are not in the way.

(vi) Scarce? How about rare, in that we seek the qualities of the Lord Jesus.

(vii) Pure- 24 karat Christians. Now and then we read news stories of those who have let down Christian standards. How these harm the Church.

(viii) Royal. 1 Peter ch 2 v 9, 'But you are a chosen people, a royal priesthood, a holy nation, a people belonging to God, that you may declare the praises of Him who called you out of darkness into His wonderful light.' Soldiers of King Jesus.

And, finally, we must not forget the Golden Rule, 'Do to others *as* you would have them do to you.' Luke ch 6 v 31 . Matthew adds 'for this sums up the Law and the Prophets.' Matthew ch 7 v 12.

Chapter 12
The Early Church in Action

Acts ch 3 v 1-20

A bit of early church history! When Jesus had been crucified, the disciples were broken men. The man in whom they placed all their hopes was dead. They had given up everything for Him, now it was all over. They had experienced three years of wonder, healing, teaching. They were anticipating a glorious victory. They had been part of an elite group of men. It seemed that they had been destined to rule the world, but Jesus was dead. They had seen Him taken. They were scared and now the authorities would be looking for them. All hopes shattered. They were scared, ashamed, they had done nothing to stop the authorities. On the road to Emmaus, one of the disciples had said 'but we had hoped that He was the One who was going to redeem Israel'.

But now it has all changed again. Jesus revealed Himself to them. He wasn't dead. He was alive. I should say 'He is alive'.

Let's pause here. There are people who do not believe that Jesus is alive. Indeed, there are people who don't believe that Jesus ever lived. It is amazing what some people believe. There are some people who do not believe that the holocaust happened and that took place just over 60 years ago. The New Testament was written a matter of a generation after the events recorded actually happened. Indeed, the N.T. records the accounts of eyewitnesses and in addition there are literally thousands of other manuscripts which stand as evidence for the life, death and resurrection of Jesus.

Moreover, Paul writes in 1 Cor. 15 v 12-22. For Christians, the resurrection of Jesus is absolutely essential to our faith. Jesus is alive. Christianity is not a faith where people strive to lead good lives, a faith based on high moral values of human conduct it is far more than that. It is a faith where men and women and boys and girls surrender their lives to the Lord Jesus Christ and allow Him to take over and live in their hearts and lives. Galatians ch 2 v 20,21.

So much for an introduction! So, we see Peter and John going up to the Temple to pray at 3 pm. There was a crippled man, sitting daily and begging. Peter said, 'Look at us'. Verses 6-10.

Our first observation from this story is the change in the disciples. From being defeated, disillusioned, despairing, they have evolved by the coming of the Holy Spirit into being bold, daring and powerful. There was the cripple, healed, walking, jumping, praising God. Everyone knew him and they too were astonished.

How did it happen? There is an explanation in v.12. Peter says 'Why do you stare at us? We didn't do it.' Yes, a miracle has been performed, but here is our second observation. Peter and John were merely channels. This miracle had been performed by Jesus. More evidence that He is alive, and they did not fail to tell everyone about it. Verses 12-20.

The authorities are alarmed. A few weeks ago, they had crucified the man, Jesus Christ. They had thought that that was the end of the matter. But, now the disciples have cured a man whom everyone knows. They could not deny that it had happened. They cannot secure false witnesses this time. But they still arrested Peter and John. Ch 4 v 1-7. So here are Peter and John, two humble fishermen standing in the midst of the Sanhedrin, the supreme court of Jerusalem made up of 71 of the most important, intellectual, wealthiest, powerful men in Jerusalem, rulers, elders, teachers of the Law and the High Priests. It was the court which had condemned Jesus. What on earth were Peter and John doing there?

Verses 8-12. This speech of Peter's must be classed as one of the most courageous speeches of all time. Here was the man who had only recently denied his Lord, pulling no punches reminding the Council what they had done.

The authorities were amazed, verses 13-17. They had witnessed the power of Jesus working through them. The once cripple was standing there. Verses 18-20 Peter and John knew what they had to do, verse 33. Peter and John became champions of the Gospel – our third observation.

They had been changed, they had become channels and now were champions for Jesus.

Where do you fit into this story?

Are you proud to be identified with Jesus? Are you one of His champions? It isn't always easy but it is a most satisfying experience to be identified with Jesus. Let's remind ourselves. We are not saying that we are followers of the greatest man whoever lived. We are saying that we have given Him, the One who showed us what God is like, our hearts and lives.

Are you happy to be a channel? Denney said in our preaching or talking that we cannot at one and the same time show that we are clever and that Christ is wonderful. We have to choose between the two. Let's just be channels.

Or, perhaps, you have not yet been changed by the grace of the Lord Jesus. He loves you, He wants to enter your heart and life. All you have to do is to invite Him, seeking His forgiveness for the past and trusting Him for the future.

Chapter 13
Paul goes into Europe

Philippi Acts ch 16 v 6-15, 16-34 and 35-40

Philippi was founded by Philip Macedon in 350 BC who was the father of Alexander the Great. It is in northern Greece and became an important Roman colony in Europe. Paul went to Philippi with Luke, Silas and Timothy in response to a vision. A man from Macedonia was crying 'Come over and help us'. It was Paul's second missionary journey. Paul normally first visited the local synagogue, but there was none. But, he found a group of women gathered together for prayer by a riverside.

Lydia, a seller of purple and possibly cloth, accepted Paul's message of salvation and opened her home to Paul and his three companions. She was apparently a lady who was comfortably off being able to provide accommodation for the four men. Lydia was the first convert in Europe but not the first European convert, as she was from Thyatira in present day Turkey.

Paul and Silas found opposition in Philippi mainly because, in the course of their preaching, they healed a young slave girl (who may well have been the first European to be converted) who brought money to her owners by fortune telling. On being healed, her owners had lost their income so they dragged Paul and Silas before the local magistrates, who severely flogged Paul and Silas and threw them into prison.

So, how do we find them in prison? Wallowing in self-pity? Not on your life. At midnight, they had a sing song

- and they brought the house down! There was an earthquake. The jailer was going to kill himself having lost, as he thought, his charges but Paul assured him that no one had left the jail - no one had escaped! The jailer and his family were saved.

In the morning, the magistrates sent officers to release Paul and Silas. Do you think they left the prison? No! The magistrates had made an awful blunder. They had flogged Roman citizens and now pleaded with the disciples to leave the place quietly.

Here then, we are introduced to three Philippians: Lydia, the slave girl and the jailer. Did Paul have them in mind when he wrote the letter to the Philippians from prison in Rome?

Philippians ch 2 v 5-11

Here in Paul's letter, we find a beautiful song of praise. Some think that Paul may have borrowed it from someone else. I like to think that it was his own composition because he does not acknowledge another and because we know from his writings that he had the ability to compose beautiful verses - think of the love chapter, his verses in Romans, there are countless examples.

v.6 We are introduced to the greatness and glory of Jesus - being in the nature of God. This is, of course, before Jesus came as a baby into the world. He had existed from the beginning. He created the world, the universe.

v.7 But, He made Himself nothing. He came to earth as a man but not just a man, a servant or slave.

v.8 A servant who was obedient - obedient to death - and no ordinary death; death on a cross. 'The death of unimaginable pain and utter shame' So from the highest to the very lowest.

v.9 But, that is not the end of the story. It is apparently as far as many people are concerned! Therefore, God exalted Him to the highest place - the very highest place- with a name above every name.

v.10 And every knee should bow in Heaven and earth.

v.11 and every tongue confess that Jesus is Lord - to the Glory of God the Father.

So, what is Paul saying to us and to Lydia, the slave girl and the jailer? Your attitude should be the same as that of Jesus Christ, Our Lord and Saviour. There was disunity and discord in Philippi. If we accept the attitude of Jesus, there is no room for that. Was Jesus thinking of Lydia, refined and generous, but needing to be reminded of the virtue of humility. The slave girl - from the lowest form of human life - used and abused. Did she need to be reminded of the depths to which Jesus had gone? He knew how she felt. He had been there. Or, the jailer - he'd nearly killed himself, but then had found something, Someone to live for. John Stott said 'The needs of human beings do not change much with the changing years, but Jesus Christ can meet them and fulfil all aspirations'. Our three needed to be free and they all found that freedom in Jesus. Chapter 4 v 4-9

Chapter 14
Origen

During the Severan persecution in AD 202. which affected the North African churches particularly, Clement, head of the Christian School, was forced to flee from Alexandria. In his absence, Origen came to prominence although only 17 years old. His own father was martyred with a few others but Origen was saved but left to provide for his mother and six younger brothers - according to the ecclesiastical historian, Eusebius.

We are advised that many strange and extravagant embellishments were written about the saints during these days. one such being Origen's self-mutilation in order to become a eunuch for the Lord's sake.

Origen was an obviously gifted disciple. He was always in demand by heathen enquirers. He learned Hebrew, began to write profusely and was made head of the catechetical school by Bishop Demetrius. A wealthy Christian named Ambrose who was converted with Origen's help, provided shorthand writers and a stream of treatises and commentaries poured from Origen's pen. Epiphanius credits Origen with output of 6,000 volumes! His works can be divided into three classes: Biblical - very many commentaries, Miscellaneous - including many letters. and Doctrinal - including two special works: Contra Celsum, a reply to a man who set out to rubbish Christian thought, but to whom Origen replied with great intellect and restraint and the De Principiis, the first great Christian theological synthesis.

Origen's relationship with Demetrius, Bishop of Alexandria, became very strained. Origen was much in demand by many churches and travelled extensively. On one occasion, he was ordained to the priesthood at Caesarea, to the dismay of Demetrius who managed to declare the ordination invalid by a group of bishops.

Origen always sought to protect the faith from heresy and many famous people came under his influence, including Gregory of Thaumaturgus later to be bishop of Neocaesarea. He was not without his critics both then and now, but he left a wonderful legacy of learning which continues to provide bases for discussion and study.

Under the persecution of Emperor Decius, Origen was imprisoned and tortured and died a few years later in AD 254. It was said of Origen, "no name of equal lustre appears in the records of the early church".

Chapter 15
Noah's weakness and others

Some years ago, a friend, Moira Wright, sent me the following from New Zealand.

The next time you feel like GOD can't use you, just remember:

Noah was a drunk

Abraham was too old

Isaac was a daydreamer

Jacob was a liar

Leah was ugly

Joseph was abused

Moses had a stuttering problem

Gideon was afraid

Samson had long hair and was a womanizer

Rahab was a prostitute

Jeremiah and Timothy were too young

David had an affair and was a murderer

Elijah was suicidal

Isaiah preached naked

Jonah ran from God

Naomi was a widow

Job went bankrupt

John the Baptist ate bugs

Peter denied Christ

The Disciples fell asleep while praying

Martha worried about everything

Mary Magdalene was, well you know

The Samaritan woman was divorced, more than once

Zaccheus was too small

Paul was too religious

Timothy had an ulcer.. .AND

Lazarus was dead!

...no more excuses now. God can use you to your full potential. Besides, you aren't the message, you are just the messenger.

Share this with a friend or two...

Chapter 16
Ephesians Chapter one v 15-23

The letter to the Ephesians

This letter is called the Queen of the Epistles. Coleridge called it the divinest composition of man - the closest to God. William Barclay said 'it shines with an even more radiant light and is clad with an even greater importance.' Paul wrote it while in prison, so he probably had more time to gather his thoughts. In chapter 3, he describes himself as the prisoner of Christ.

Scholars believe that it was not actually written directly to the Ephesians but was a circular letter for all the churches. Why do they think that? Paul spent three years in Ephesus and loved the church there wholeheartedly and they also loved him. His other letters contain nearly always various personal notes to specific friends. In this letter there is an absence of such notes and it does not seem possible therefore that the letter was specific to the Ephesians. Read Acts ch 20 last verse.

Just now, we are looking at Ch 1 verses 15-23. We often hear sermons based on love, peace, joy and the fruits of the spirit. We are looking now at more unusual virtues which Paul writes about.

WISDOM. The Greek word for wisdom is Sophia. Paul is telling us here that we need to be a thinking people. James Boswell, the 18th century writer said something like: If my shoes need attention, I take them to the shoe repairer, if my coat needs attention, I take it to the tailor, if my religion needs attention I go to the priest. That just is not good enough. We are responsible for our own spiritual condition. We need to pray, to study the word - and that takes time. We probably all fail to meet the time necessary to keep our spirits in good trim. And by the way wisdom is not the same as education. For education we go to school and if possible college, for wisdom we go to God. Maybe, we just do not spend as much time with the Lord as we ought.

William Barclay criticised the church for spending hours on mundane problems of administration and little time on theological matters. We need to gain a deeper wisdom of the things of God. And, that comes from prayer and the Word. Christians should grow in wisdom, knowledge and grace, for if we do not grow closer to God over the years, our experience of God will suffer.

We are all familiar with natural revelation. The earth, flowers, animals, the sun, sky and stars - Romans ch 1 v 20. But we need spiritual revelation from the Word of God.

HOPE. Do you think we are living in an age of despair? We read our papers, watch TV and almost shudder at the things that are going on. The state of the prisons, the National Health Service, Mental Health issues, Education and we could go on. 'In the world you shall have tribulation, but be of good cheer, I have overcome the world'. We have hope.

Hope is a strange word. The noun and the verb seem to have different meanings. Let us look at the verb: I hope that West Ham (English football) will win their next football match! Young people hope to pass their next exams. I hope that this article will have a good outcome, that someone will take it into their heart or maybe I should start again! The future is uncertain. But, the noun is completely different. The noun hope means expectation, assurance, promise. Someone used the phrase: 'As hopeful as the break of day'. It is certain. Hope is the opposite of despair. It is an optimistic attitude of mind that is based on an expectation of positive outcomes. The Christian hope is a strong and confident expectation of a Heavenly outcome. Roman ch 15 v 13, 1 Corinthians ch 15 v 19,20 and 1 Timothy ch 1 v 1.

Application: We can be inspired by these words but do not keep them to yourselves. It is not a question of 'I'm alright Jack'. This is the message we need to share with our brothers and sisters outside the church. Someone wrote: 'By life and word, we can make sure that those around us clearly understand what it is to follow Christ. They may call themselves non-Christians but they are among those for whom Christ died. It has been suggested that we ought to think of unbelievers that we know and meet not as non-Christians but as not yet Christians.'

Chapter 17
Ephesians Ch 4

Humility, Gentleness, Patience and Love.

Humility

What is your vocabulary like? How many words do you know? probably, a lot more than you think. A few years ago, research was done which estimated the size of an average person's vocabulary. But, it was very difficult. For instance, half-hearted, is that one word or two. E.g. for example, is that two words? There are many problems. Anyway, the research showed roughly that a two-year-old had a vocabulary of about 300 words, a five-year-old about 5,000 words and a 12-year-old about 12,000 words. This was a very rough estimate. (I don't think it showed if a woman had a greater one than a man!) An adult had perhaps 12000 plus. Another source thought about 10,000 words for an adult. One person believed that Shakespeare has a vocabulary of 30,000 words.

The trouble is that new words are being added all the time. Do you remember Catherine Tate: 'Am I bovvered'. Believe it or not the word bovver is now in the Oxford English Dictionary! There are many other examples, like air punch, solar farm, sick notes and, of course, the new language of texting: LOL? Laugh out loud or Lots of Love! BRB Be right back, GTG Got to go and JK Just kidding......

Why all this information about words? In Paul's day the language was Greek and Christianity increased the number of words because Jesus brought into life virtues which were previously unknown.

New words were needed to describe the new virtues which Jesus' faith brought. 'So completely is the idea of human brotherhood due to Christianity that Max Muller, an expert in languages, informs us that the very word humanity was unknown before Christianity.' Humanism ought to take note of that. William Barclay writes: 'It has been said that chastity was a new virtue which Christianity introduced into the world. Women were treated as mere objects. The ancient world regarded sexual immorality as no sin at all. Even the Jew gave thanks to God that He had not been made him a gentile, slave or woman. We have so much to thank Jesus for and for the wonderful way Jesus used women in His ministry. Where would the Salvation Army be without the service of its women. Yet there are still churchmen who do not recognise the true place of women in the church.

In our reading from Ephesians, Paul writes about four virtues: humility, gentleness, patience and love.

Most of this chapter will be taken up with the study of humility as here again, there was no word in the Greek language for humility - not as we know it today.

First, humility, what it isn't. In Paul's day, humility was a cowering, cringing quality to be despised, not to be desired. Do you remember Uriah Heap in the Charles Dickens story? He revelled in his humility and grovelling. We can be proud of our humility. "I'm humble, I'm humble as humble as can be. The greatest thing about me is my humility!'

Do you compare yourself with others? I suppose we all do in a way. I can play the piano, but if I do, you would have to sing very very slowly. Occasionally, Diane, my wife, and I have a walk on the beach. I think I am observant, but I never see anything of interest, whereas Diane will be picking up things to show me. We gather self-knowledge all the time.

I think we often think about ourselves, perhaps doing wonderful things like winning gold medals, Wimbledon, rescuing someone, scoring a wonderful goal for England. But do we imagine or day dream that we are humble? Edith Sitwell (Dame and poet) is recorded as saying: 'I have often wished I had time to cultivate modesty.....but I am too busy thinking about myself.' On the other hand, John Ruskin (artist and art critic) said: 'I believe the first test of a truly great man is his humility.' William A. Ward was an American who wrote inspirational maxims for instance: 'A warm smile is the universal language of kindness' and 'Today is a most unusual day, because we have never lived it before and we will never live it again, it is the only day we have.' He wrote, coming back to humility: 'He is without humility who sees it in himself.'

It is said that humility is the virtue on which all others depend. And Confucius said: 'It is the solid foundation of all virtues.'

When we come to thinking about Jesus, comparison is not difficult, it is impossible. Jesus is perfect. Christian humility comes from seeing your life in the light of Jesus. We become aware of self-knowledge. We know that we are inadequate but we also know that we are in Christ. We are comfortable with who we are in Christ.

Gentleness

Kind, understanding, merciful - what qualities! Of course, seen again in Jesus. We can argue all day about religion, whatever that is, and get nowhere, but there is no argument about kindness, especially when it is not expected. William Barclay, with his knowledge of Greek, says that a gentle person is one under control. His every instinct, every passion, every motion of mind, heart, tongue and desire are under perfect control. Then he will be God's perfect gentleman.

Patience

Or long suffering. Paul was, of course, a Roman citizen. In his day, the Romans were unconquerable. They could not think of losing a war. They would never give in. Christian patience is the spirit which will never admit defeat. On the Greek side, patience is the spirit which refuses to retaliate. Have you seen a large dog worried by a small puppy? The puppy will growl, bite, irritate, the large dog will take it all with a calm dignity, without complaint.-Martin Luther said something like, if the world had treated me like it has treated God, I would have kicked into oblivion years ago.'

Love

Here once again, the Greeks had difficulty with Christian love. There were three normal words for love. They had EROS which was a word used to describe the love between a man and his sweetheart, they had the word STORGE which described family love and the word PHILIA warm affection between friends. Wm Barclay writes: Christian love was something so new that the Christian writers had to invent a word for it or at least they had to take a word which was a very unusual Greek word, the word AGAPE. It means a love which will seek the highest good in others no matter what they may do. It is a quality not of the emotions but of the will. It is a love which will seek the highest good of the unlovely, unlovable and those who do not love us. It is the power to love even people we do not like. Once again, we see this, of course. in Jesus.

Jesus did literally turn the world upside down and we, as followers of Jesus, must continue this mission. Are you up for it?

Chapter 18
Women in the Church

In Paul's day, the place of women in society was very low. William Barclay quotes the Talmud (the body of Jewish Civil and Ceremonial law) which lists, among the plagues of the world 'the talkative and the inquisitive widow and the virgin who wastes her time in prayers'. The male Jew, in his morning prayers, thanked God that he had not made him a Gentile, a slave or a woman. Women took no part in the synagogue service. They were not allowed to teach in a school. To teach the law to a woman was to 'cast pearls before swine'. The strict Rabbi was not allowed to speak to women in the street. This was the society in which Paul grew up and worked. In addition, we need to consider the Greek society of Corinth.

Greek society was even more complex for the women for they were either respectable or the victims of society through being poor or caught up in the doubtful religious practices of various temples e.g. Aphrodite of Corinth. Even the respectable Greek woman would never been seen in the street alone. She would be confined to her own quarters, would not be allowed to speak or take part in any public assembly.

It is hardly surprising then that Paul would write to the church in Corinth that women should remain silent (1 Corinthians 14 v 34). Paul was trying to establish orderly worship and he had to be careful about how the church would be seen. It would have been so easy to cause misunderstanding. The silence then of women was more a need of society than any religious or theological instruction.

When the Holy Spirit was poured out on the early church, Peter addressed the crowds with words from the prophet Joel: 'In the last days, God says, I will pour out my Spirit on all people. Your sons and *daughters* will prophesy, your young men will see visions, your old men will dream dreams. Even on my servants, both men and *women*, I will pour out my Spirit........' This seems clear enough. Jesus used women in so many ways. First of all, He was born to Mary, a most saintly lady. He was subject *to* both Mary and Joseph (Luke 2 v 51). The women ministered to Jesus throughout His ministry, they comforted Jesus at Cavalry. The first person to discover the risen Saviour was Mary Magdalene. Into the life of the early church, it was Priscilla and Aquila (note the order) who instructed Apollos. In the sad difference of Euodia and Syntyche (both women), they were fellow labourers in the Gospel (Philippians 4 v 2, 3). Paul stayed with Philip who had four unmarried daughters who prophesied (Acts 21 v 8). In Titus, he advises the older women to teach what is good (Titus 2 v 3). Paul himself mentions so many women in Romans 16, a most fascinating chapter, starting with Phoebe, a servant of the church.

As a Salvationist, all this is most acceptable. The founders of The Salvation Army were William and Catherine Booth. Catherine's inspiration resulted in so many wonderful women leaders, officers and soldiers in the 'Army'. Finally, as Paul himself writes (Galatians 3 v 28): 'There is neither Jew nor Greek, slave nor free, male nor female, for you are all one in Christ Jesus.' So, we certainly pray for women bishops.

Chapter 19
Psalm 23

St. John ch 10 v 1 – 18 Isaiah ch 53 v 4 – 9

All human life is found in the few verses of Psalm 23. It starts with a most positive declaration 'The Lord is MY Shepherd'. It is a Psalm of David. When Samuel was looking for the next King of Israel, David was taking care of the sheep. He knew what a shepherd was. He had risked his life protecting his sheep. He had fought with lions and bears and after his experience serving his God and his country, he is able to say The Lord is my Shepherd. (1 Samuel ch 17 v33-37)

We read in St John ch 10 that the sheep know His voice and He knows His sheep by name. We are reading here of our Almighty God, the Father, creator, preserver and governor of Heaven and earth. He knows his sheep by name.

When someone joins the forces, one of the first things to happen is the giving of a number. Mine was 2495059 - after over nearly 70 years since doing my National Service, the number is firmly in my memory.

What other numbers do we have? National Insurance, N.H.S., bank numbers galore and they get longer - telephone, electricity, gas, water, various membership numbers. Why do we have so many? It's been argued that we could all individually have just one number for everything, but that is too simple. The Good Shepherd knows His sheep by name.

'It is enough that Christ goes with us on our journey.' Donald English.

'I shall not be in want' We do not need anything else. My Lord is all sufficiency. Verses 2 and 3 draw a delightful picture. There is rest, guidance, restoration. The Psalm has been called a 'lyrical gem'. It confirms God's desire that we should find pleasure in His world. It is right to rest and relax. Obviously, this could be taken too far and there are dangers here, but that should not hinder or detract from the proper and legitimate pursuit of pleasure and relaxation. It is after all recreation.

Now, when life throws its worst at us - verse 4 - He is there to comfort, support and strengthen. 'I will fear no evil for you are with me.' We live in a suffering world.

I will not presume to know the answer to the suffering of the world, but with the help of the Rev Peter Brooks, can I offer some thoughts.

We have been sickened over the years by various tragedies. What is the answer? In St. Luke ch 13 v 1 - 5, we read of two tragedies, one where men had butchered others and secondly where there was some kind of accident. They were brought to the attention of Jesus. The orthodox Jewish view was that these men had sinned in some terrible way. Jesus contradicted this view. It is not that kind of world. Jesus says in St Matt ch 10 v 29 'Are not two sparrows sold for a penny? Yet not one of them will fall to the ground apart from the will of your Father'. Peter Brooks says 'It does not follow that God selects sparrow A to cop it and sparrow B to survive, but it does mean that the whole process of life and death is contained within His will. It is a world in which tragic accidents can happen, but it is God's world; everything is contained within His purpose......People say, 'If I'd designed the world, I'd have made it without any pain in it.' Their compassion is splendid especially if it moves them to action but..... perhaps their painless world would never have produced their concern for others. (Chapter one also deals a little with this aspect of life).

We find it hard to imagine a world without pain and suffering. Would it also be a world without emotion, feeling, compassion, care, love?

I believe that God suffers when His creatures suffer and after all let us not forget that this world is not the end. When we die, we go into God's presence. Romans ch 8 v 39.

Verse 5. One commentator has suggested that there are lots of references to food throughout the Bible. Joseph was the provider of food, we have the feeding of the 5000, parables of the great supper, the marriage feast of the Bridegroom etc. etc. and here we have the provision of food even in the presence of enemies.

Running over, running over my cup's full and running over. This Psalm is not just for funerals.

And finally, verse 6. Heaven begins here on earth and continues above. Yes, we have all human life in these verses, plus eternal life. Thank you, Lord, for all your provision. Help us so to live that we may help others to find you as their Shepherd too.

Chapter 20
Home

Home: is the place where you can enjoy corn on the cob, soup and spaghetti... is the place where when you go to it, they have to take you in! Home is the place where you wait until your son/daughter brings home the car.

It has been said that nothing bugs a woman more than friends who drop in to see the home as it really is.

A happy home is where a wife asks her husband's opinion and accepts it!

Enough of this frivolity.......Lets be more serious. How often have you said, 'I wish I was at home'? We want to be in familiar surroundings, we want to relax, kick off our shoes (undo our corsets!) get in the favourite chair.... ' Aaahh....'

We have been told that in the ideal family, we find a mother and father and 2.5 children!! But, it isn't an ideal world. Every November most of us join the Remembrance Service in the Royal Albert Hall in London - the bit that gets me is when the widows come down the steps, some only recently widowed. It certainly isn't an ideal world.

Jesus was fortunate in His upbringing. Mary and Joseph created a home for Him and His brothers and sisters. We read, 'He went down to Nazareth with them and was obedient to them...and Jesus grew in wisdom and stature, and in favour with God and man.' (Luke ch 2). But, it is assumed that unfortunately Joseph died sometime in

Jesus' youth as there is no record of Joseph being present at the wedding in Cana. Mary from the first knew that it was not an ideal world.

How do you think Jesus acted at home? I can imagine His diligence at home and work. I can imagine His witnessing some injustice down in the market but reluctantly holding Himself back because His time had not yet come. That must have been difficult. Personally, I don't think Jesus was a goody goody two shoes. I can imagine Him teasing His mother and their laughing together but doing everything in love.

How do we behave at home? Michael Griffiths writes that it is better for a son to miss reading his Bible if it means he neglects helping his mother with the chores. It is possible to put spiritual duties before giving practical help which is genuinely needed. We can use anything as an excuse to get out of doing valuable work. Do you agree?

Brother Lawrence said he sought God's presence constantly whether he was worshipping in the church or working in the kitchen. The time of business does not differ from the time of prayer. We can worship the Lord in any situation.

We may feel sometimes that family life is being attacked in this crazy world. Let us be determined to protect our families and always remember that you are not alone. The Lord Jesus is with you by His Holy Spirit and there are millions of Christians just like you playing their part all round the world.

Do you remember poor old Elijah? He suffered amazingly a period of depression after a great victory. 'I am the only one left and now they are trying to kill me too.' The Lord said, 'I reserve seven thousand in Israel - all whose knees have not bowed down to Baal.' We are never alone.

Family life in Paul's days was precarious. William Barclay writes, 'When a child was born, the child was taken and laid at the father's feet. If the father lifted up the child that meant he acknowledged it. If he turned away and left it the child was literally thrown away. There was never a night when there were thirty or forty abandoned children left in the Roman forum.' The father's power was absolute. A son never came of age, he was always under the control of his father.

Some of you have been adopted. In Roman law adoption was a very serious and difficult step. The absolute possession had to pass in a complex series of steps and afterwards the result was (1) the son lost all rights to the old family (2) he became heir to his new father's estate (3) his old life was completely wiped out and (4) the adopted son was literally and absolutely the son of his new father.

Why have we been looking at Roman family life in this detail? Romans ch 8 v 13-17. We began our worship thinking of family life, we now think about God's family. We are no longer slaves to sin with no hope, no future, we have been, through Jesus' love and sacrificial death and resurrection welcomed into God's family, not as servants or slaves but as sons and daughters of God Our Father. We are heirs of God, joint heirs with Christ. I wish I had the ability and words to convey what all this means. But, what does Paul say about it: verse 18. Like Roman adoption, the past is cancelled and wiped out, we are adopted into God's family and share in His Glory. Sometime ago, I was moaning about something, I can't remember what...and I said to myself, why me, why do I have to do that? Then I thought, what would Jesus say? He would say, what more can I do? When we think of our inheritance and what it cost, what more can we do?

Chapter 21
Demons

A few thoughts on this subject from many different sources:

It would seem that from the time of Jesus' experience in the wilderness, the conflict between Jesus and Satan seriously began. Jesus had made it clear that He was against all that Satan stood for and as we progress through Jesus' ministry, we become convinced of His ultimate victory- over Satan, sin, pain, suffering and death. St John ch 16 v 33 'In the world you will have trouble. But take heart, I have overcome the world.' Demon possession is just a part of this great struggle.

Do demons exist? Christians have the Holy Spirit and the Lord has certainly used angels in His plans. Satan similarly may well have his assistants. There is plenty of testimony from those who have cast out demons (particularly in the Charismatic churches) and there is plenty of testimony from those who have been delivered from demons. However, there are those who seem to attribute to demons all kinds of problems including physical ailments. Some seek demons for all pastoral problems which means that the individual is able to avoid personal responsibility for his actions. It would seem that we can go too far in this direction. At the same time, to dismiss demon possession is too easy a solution.

The Gospels make a clear distinction between sickness and demon possession. St. Matt ch 10 v 1, St Mark ch 6 v 13 and St Luke ch 9 v 1. Perhaps, today, we would refer to mental illness, when considering the demonic type of behaviour. There are many mysteries in life particularly relating to human behaviour and for all the benefit of modern science, we do not seem to be much nearer to explaining and/or analysing such phenomena.

But, we have to be aware of the dangers hinted at by C.E.B. Cranfield that the greatest achievement of the powers of evil would be to persuade us that they do not exist.

In Jesus' days, nervous diseases and insanity were seen as due to evil possession. This does not mean that Jesus dogmatically taught that it was fact but, He did seem to accommodate the theory. Why? (1) The 'sick' person who was looking for healing would be convinced that he was possessed and (2) Jesus did not wish, at that moment, to unnecessarily interfere with the beliefs of His time. The beliefs of demon possession were so near the truth that for most purposes of practical religion, it might be regarded as true. (In any case, look at the lack of progress we have made since then).

What then do we need to remember about this subject? (i) If Jesus can enter the human heart, then cannot Satan and his demons do the same? There have been so many examples of evil behaviour - is there any other explanation? (ii) God can free the human heart from such invasions. (iii) Jesus is supreme and has won the victory and finally (iv) the Holy Spirit empowers human beings to live lives free from Satan's power- Romans ch 8 v 28 - 39.

A slightly different slant on demons: St. Mark ch- 9 v 38- 42

At the time of Jesus, people believed in demons. They believed that illnesses, mental and physical, were caused by demons. The disciples heard that a man, unknown to the company of Jesus, was casting out demons in the name of Jesus. How could this be? There was a common way of exorcising demons. If the exorcist could come up with a more powerful spirit, he could command the demon to leave the sufferer. This man was using the name of Jesus, the all powerful name and so he was being successful. Jesus said that if he was using His name, then he must be for Me. 'He who is not against Me is for Me.'

'Every man has a right to his own thoughts.' I cannot tell you what to think, you cannot tell me what to think. We all need to come to our own conclusions and we all need to respect other people even with different conclusions, not only what they believe but also what they say. Voltaire laid down the idea of freedom of speech when he said, 'I hate what you say but I would die for your right to say it.'

Like the disciples, we are always ready to condemn what we do not understand. William Barclay said, 'It is a common fault amongst Christians to make judgements about things we do not understand.' He also said that there are two things which we should remember:

1. There is far more than one way to God. For many years, I had little time for Jehovah's Witnesses. I would welcome an argument. Now, I know that between us and them, there are theological differences. They do not accept Jesus as part of the Godhead and they refuse to accept

the Holy Trinity, but if a sincere JW has found God in his/her congregation, who am I to belittle their faith. A friend of mine always use to hire JWs to clean her house because they were so thorough in their work. My attitude today is that I tell them it is a great shame that we cannot have fellowship and worship God together. You know, there are certain Christians who believe that if a person has not heard about Jesus, then they are doomed. I believe that if a person has lived according to the light that they have received, then the Lord will judge them accordingly. I often think about people who have been deeply hurt by the behavior of so-called Christians/priests/ minsters.

2. We must also remember that truth is always bigger than a man's grasp of it. What is truth? This is where toleration comes in. John Morley wrote, 'Toleration means reverence for all the possibilities of truth. . ..it means frank respect for freedom of indwelling conscience.. .it means the charity that is greater than faith or hope.'

    William Barclay said, 'Intolerance is a sign of arrogance and ignorance, for it is a sign that there is no truth beyond the truth that a man sees.' Therefore, we must concede the right to every man/woman the right to do his own thinking and his own speaking. The speaking part can have its limitations. If a message threatens to destroy morality, to destroy the foundation of civilised society, then the message should be challenged and proved to be wrong.

Chapter 22
Constantine the Great

After the chaos caused by the resignation of Diocletian, Constantine, son of Constantius, was proclaimed emperor by his troops in York in 306. Thus began his rise to power.

Galerius was still dominant in the east pursuing the Christians but both poor health and opposition finally defeated him. On his death bed in 311, he signed an edict of toleration, blaming the previous troubles on the behavior of the Christians and at the same time asking for their prayers. Regretfully following the death of Galerius, his successor, Maximin continued the reign of terror but after a short time was forced to flee by Licinius.

The year 312. saw a most significant event which was to have a powerful effect on European if not world history. Constantine's remaining rival was Maxentius. Their armies met at the Milvian Bridge. During the previous night. Constantine believed he saw a vision of a cross of light. He ordered his soldiers to put a Christian monogram on their shields. In the following battle, Constantine won. For the first time. Rome had an Augustus, if not a committed Christian at that time, one who was most sympathetic towards them.

Rome now was ruled jointly by Constantine in the west and Licinius in the east. They met in Milan to issue an edict of religious freedom throughout the empire to which Licinius was not faithful. However, peace ruled in the west and Constantine offered generous help to the churches.

It has been noted that at this time the Roman coin still bore the symbol of the sun, perhaps revealing a gradual move towards his personal conversion to Christianity by Constantine. From 320. the sun symbol was dropped and soldiers had to attend compulsory church parades. In 321, Constantine made Sunday a public holiday.

During this time while the west was enjoying peace, the rule of Licinius deteriorated. Constantine at first was unable to interfere, but an opportunity came when barbarians broke across the Danube and Constantine went to help. With the danger out of the way, the two rulers fell out. This resulted in the defeat of Licinius at the battle of Chrysopolis. So, after years of civil war, the empire was reunited in 324 and Constantine became the sole Augustus.

Rome became a united empire, with a new Emperor, a new capital (Byzantine) and a new religion.

(Was Constantine a 'truly committed' Christian? I think we can conclude that only Constantine and the Lord know the answer. His behaviour towards his son Crispus and wife Fausta obviously introduce a dark cloud of doubt but there can be no denying the tremendous boost the faith received from Constantine's legislative programmes and building projects. 'Eusebius confirmed what Constantine himself believed; that he had a special and personal relationship with the Christian God.')

Chapter 23
Islam

Islam means surrender or submission to the will of God.
A follower of Islam is called a muslim. Muslims believe
that muslims have always existed, but only came to light
after Muhammad who was born around AD 570 in
Mecca. They believe that he was the last and greatest
prophet - others included Abraham, Moses and Jesus
and the other O.T. prophets. Mecca, the centre of Islam,
is in Arabia roughly in the centre of present day Saudi
Arabia. Medina another important town is about 200
miles north of Mecca.

When Muhammad was born both towns were on busy
caravan routes. They were religious centres before
Muhammad was born. In Mecca there is a holy place, an
ancient temple, called Kabah which includes the Black
Stone (7" in diameter), the centre of religious pilgrimages
many years before Muhammad. It can be said that Islam
is a reformation of older religions with new material
added. Of course the centre of their faith is now Allah
whilst before Muhammad there were many idols in the
Kabah. Muhammad's father died before he was born
and his mother died 6 years afterwards. He was brought
up by his uncle Abu Talib, who trained him to be a
merchant. When he was 25 years old he married a
wealthy widow called Kadijah who was 40 years of age,
but they had six children, though sadly the two boys did
not survive. (One daughter, Fatima later married the 4th
Caliph – chief muslim).

When forty, Muhammad began to prophecy. Muslims
believe he was visited by the angel Gabriel. At this time,

it was said of Muhammad that he was a competent trader, wary general and thoughtful administrator. It has also been said that he could not read or write but that he recited what he had been told by Gabriel. Of, course this was the beginning of the Koran or Qu'ran. (The Koran is divided into 114 chapters called surahs).

Young people and poor men were attracted to his religious beliefs and later an important man named Abu Bakr joined bringing strength to his group. He later became the first Caliph.

As the group grew, opposition also grew in Mecca. Much of the unrest was caused by Muhammad who denounced the idols in the Kabah - he believed in one true God, Allah. Various things changed. His wife died, pilgrims came from Medina who accepted his teaching. He married the daughter of Abu Bakr. And, it became difficult to stay in Mecca, so they migrated to Medina in AD 622 where he was accepted. There had been much tribal strife in the town and he was able to bring an amount of stability to the situation. This date marks the beginning of the Muslim era. There was a big population of Jews in Medina and he tried to win them over by praying to Jerusalem, but the Jews were critical of his teaching and his poor knowledge of the Jewish Scriptures, so they prayed to Mecca. Muhammad had two aims (1) to convert all Arabia to his faith and (2) to destroy the Jews. He began to preach the duty of the Holy War. His battles against his enemies were successful and the group increased in possessions. There were many battles between Mecca and Medina and Muhammad promised Paradise to his fighters! He marched to Mecca, went to the Kabah, touched the

Black Stone, cried 'God is Great', destroyed the idols and proclaimed Allah as sole God. He died in AD 632 aged 62.

In prayers, there is much recitation from the Koran, but what is the origin of the book? It is believed that some of it is from the older religions, there is much of the Old Testament. Someone said: 'It is clear that Muhammad had not read the Old Testament for there are many differences of detail.' There is also some detail from The New Testament, but it does not appear to be direct knowledge, for instance, he believed the Trinity to be Jesus, God the Father and the Virgin Mary.

The five Pillars of Faith are: prayer - five times a day, fasting, alms, pilgrimages and profession of faith. Friday is the sacred day for males to worship. There are no images, no paintings, no pews, no music and no collections, but a fortieth of income should be given to the poor. During Ramadam (near the ninth month of the Muslim year) there should be no food or drink between sunrise and sunset and, of course, no wine or pork. Women rarely join in public worship.

After the death of Muhammad, the armies of Abu Bakr almost insensibly attacked lands beyond Arabia. After his death, there was a great deal of schism amongst the leaders but the religion spread far and wide from Spain, France to India and China. Spain turned back to Christianity in the thirteenth century. Later under the Turks, the Arab world went into stagnation for centuries.

Today, the main groups of Muslims are the Shi'ites, Sunnis, Wahhabis and the Bahais. The Shi'ites follow the Caliph Ali who was the cousin and son in-law of Muhammad and they believe he was the true Caliph, in fact he was the fourth Caliph according to the Sunnis. The Shi'ites reject the first three Caliphs. The Shi'ites are to be found in Iran, Pakistan and Yemen today. The Sunnis who are called the traditionalists are elsewhere. The Wahhabis (with Sunni influence) were founded in the eighteenth century by Al-Wahhab and live mainly in Saudi Arabia which includes Mecca and Medina. They are puritanical but the riches of oil are having an influence on the pattern of life. The Bahais, founded in the nineteenth century, seek to unite all religions and establish a worldwide brotherhood, but they have suffered much persecution from other Islamic sects.

Women are in the home for the bearing and nurturing of children. However, in these days women are acquiring more freedom. A man may have up to four wives but it appears these days one is the norm. (Muhammad had 10 wives).

I have tried to be factual in this summary of beliefs, but my conclusion must be to state that Islam has been spread by a Holy War - at times, it was believe and accept our faith or die - compared to true Christianity which has been spread by a message of love, through Our Lord Jesus Christ.

Do not confuse ordinary Muslims with the radical extremists. As Christians we should be tolerant of other faiths. How can we judge a person who feels they have found God and are trying to live a life well pleasing to Him.

BELIEF

Muslims believe in the one true God whom they call Allah.

PRAYER

Muslims are called to pray 5 times a day. Prayers are often quotes from the Koran, the Holy Book of Muslims

RAMADAN

During Ramadan (in the ninth month of the Muslim year) fasting takes place. There is no food and drink between sunrise and sunset.

CHARITY

A fortieth of a Muslim's income should be given to the poor.

PILGRIMAGE

A Muslim has a duty to make a pilgrimage to Mecca, the home of Islam, at least once in his lifetime, if he is in good health.

* * * * *

FOOD AND DRINK

No alcohol and no pork. Food should be prepared in accordance with Halal rules.

MUSLIM DRESS

For women: the Burqua is a full outer garment with just the eyes uncovered, the hijab is a head covering scarf and the nijab is a full head covering with only the eyes uncovered.

OTHER INFORMATION

Friday is the sacred day for males to worship. There are many different sects in Islam.

Chapter 24
Suffering - more thoughts.

Jesus was familiar with suffering, not just at the end of His life but His experiences before His tragic yet victorious death. His first experience of bereavement may have been the loss of his cousin. 'On Herod's birthday, the daughter of Herodias danced for them......(Matthew ch. 14 v 6) and we know how that ended up. But Jesus was constantly surrounded by sick people seeking healing. How did Jesus look upon suffering? In Luke ch 13, we have two incidents of people who had suffered - a slaughter and a disaster. In these days, the orthodox Jewish view was that people suffered because of their sinfulness and those who had suffered in the two incidents were particularly wicked. But Jesus confirmed that it was the whole nation, every single man and woman, who needed to repent. Our suffering is not necessarily caused by ourselves. It is not a result of our own sin necessarily - it can be - but it is certainly not a judgement.

We remember Jesus at the grave of Lazarus. Jesus wept. Jesus lived in the midst of life. He knew the desperate needs of people and He healed so many. He knew what is was to be like us. John ch 16 v 33 'In this world you will have tribulation. But take heart! I have overcome the world.'

The world suffers in so many ways. There are natural disasters, earthquakes, storms & floods, famines. There are wars, tragedies Aberfan - there are murders... .and when children are involved in any of these, our hearts break with grief and sorrow. We could say that everyone,

107

in one way or another, will suffer from personal tragedies, sickness, bereavement, disastrous relationships, loneliness, injustices of many kinds. Now, Christians believe in a God of love, but as Nicky Gumbel says: 'suffering is the Christian's greatest challenge to his faith and the most difficult question to answer,' but, he continues, 'there was no suffering before man rebelled against God and there will be no more suffering when God creates a new Heaven and a new earth,' (Revelation ch 21).

I believe that God is in our suffering. When we hear of a child who has died, I feel that God has taken the little one to His bosom. Regretfully, it is those who are left behind who share the sorrow.

God works through suffering. I'm sure we all know those saints who have suffered, sometimes all their lives, yet have a wonderful relationship with the Lord and He shines through them. I am always so moved by TV programmes which visit a children's ward in a hospital only to find very ill children full of fun and laughter - amazing young heroes and heroines.

Can you imagine a world without suffering? To say, in such a world, 'How are you?' would be totally unnecessary. There would be no feeling for each other, no care or support, no charities! It would be a breeding ground for indifference.

One thing we can be sure about. The Lord is with us in our suffering and we can anticipate that day when 'He will wipe every tear from their (our) eyes.'

Chapter 25
C. T. Studd

Mr. Edward Studd, father of C.T., was a retired planter who had made a fortune in India and who returned home to England to spend it! He loved sport and hunting and was Master of the Hounds. He loved horse racing and cricket and he turned his paddock into a first class cricket ground. He won several steeplechases including the Grand National. There is no doubt that in his particular environment he was top of the tree.

Edward had a friend, a Mr. Vincent, and he took Edward to a theatre nothing unusual about that except for the fact that the two men at the theatre were Moody and Sankey, two American evangelists. To cut a long story short, Edward got wonderfully saved. He lived only for a further two years but in that time he accomplished a tremendous work for the Saviour. Edward's three sons were at Eton. Edward's first job was to write to his sons in the middle of term to meet him in town. He took them to hear Mr. Moody and all three got saved. They were Kynaston, George and Charlie.

All three boys were brilliant at cricket and with their new experience, they started a Bible Class at Eton. Charlie (C.T.) was exceptional at cricket. After Eton, he went to Cambridge and he made the England team. He played with W.G. Grace and he gave his life to cricket. It wasn't just a sport or pastime; it was serious business.

So cricket became C.T.'s life, but a serious shock was awaiting round the corner. George became seriously ill. C.T. was especially close to George and he was constantly at his bedside. As he watched George hovering between life and death, C.T. thought, 'what is all the fame and flattery worth? What is it worth to possess all the riches in the world when a man comes to face eternity?' After six years of backsliding, Charlie rededicated his life to Jesus and George was restored to good health.

Then another strange thing happened. C.T. received the call to take the Gospel to China. For some reason, the rest of the family were against the idea but C.T. was determined and amazingly six other Cambridge graduates joined him and they became the Cambridge Seven.

Another shock! C.T. inherited a large fortune of £29,000 from his father. This was in 1887. C.T. was determined to give it away and he started with £25,000 (in today's money £1.25M). He gave £250,000 (today's money) to the work of The Salvation Army in India (Commissioner Booth Tucker), he sent £50,000 to General Booth, £50,000 to Bamardos and another cheque to the East End of London and then more to others.

Then it was off to China. His text was 'What shall it profit a man if he gain the whole world and lose his own soul.'

A year before C.T. arrived in China, a young lady arrived in Shanghai Priscilla Livingstone Stewart. Needless to say, C.T. and Priscilla met, fell in love and got married. Over the years, they had four beautiful daughters, Grace, Dorothy, Edith and Pauline. Before C.T. met Priscilla, he was discussing marriage with his friends. He said,

'Well, please God, I don't want to marry, but if I do, I want to marry a real Salvation Army Hallelujah lassie.'

C.T. and Priscilla obviously met all kinds of difficulties during their service. They spent ten years in China, six years in India, then at age 50 and after 15 years of poor health, twenty years in Africa. C.T. founded the World Evangelisation Crusade, which operates today in 80 countries – (W.E.C. International). He was often very ill, had no money, but trusted in His Saviour who always saw him through.

He said, 'The committee I work under is a conveniently small committee, a very wealthy committee, wonderfully generous and is always sitting in session - the committee of the Father, the Son and the Holy Spirit.'

He once said, 'I have searched into my life and do not know of anything else left that I can sacrifice to the Lord Jesus.'

Chapter 26
Thorn in the Flesh

Readings: 2 Corinthians ch 11 v 21(b)-30 and 12 v 1-10

Paul was a great man, a very great man. He had tremendous intellect. He had all the qualifications necessary for his time. He was a Jew, a Pharisee, instructed at the feet of Gamaliel, 'the most illustrious rabbi of his day, honoured by his people.' Paul was a tireless worker for the Jewish cause. He was also a Roman citizen. He was familiar with Greek philosophy, as we saw when he was in Athens.

But then, Paul had a remarkable conversion to Christianity. It was not immediate. The Lord said to him on the road to Damascus 'It is hard for you to kick against the goads.' The Holy Spirit had been at work within his heart and mind for some time, possibly since he had witnessed Stephen's martyrdom. However, on the road to Damascus, Paul yielded and committed his life to Jesus. Now, he became a tireless worker for the Lord- the Apostle to the Gentiles.

It was still sometime before Paul actually began his life's ministry. He visited Jerusalem, spent time in Arabia and then several years in Tarsus and Syria, preparing and reflecting for the future. Barnabas was a great help and eventually the two set off on the first missionary journey. They did not have an easy ride. They were constantly harassed by troublemakers who were Jews who would not accept the Gospel as taught by Paul and Barnabas. They followed Paul around, travelling hundreds of miles in order to stir up opposition. Paul called them false apostles, deceitful workers, Judaisers, who insisted that Gentile converts should be circumcised, bringing the old baggage of the Law into the new Gospel.

The church at Corinth was suffering and Paul felt he had to write. In his second letter, he felt that he had to set out his qualifications and experience. He did not like to boast but in the first reading above, he lists some of his exploits: he received lashes five times, beaten with rods three times, shipwrecked three times etc. We know so little of his experiences, but then in the next chapter he mentions a very deep spiritual experience. The third Heaven is a Jewish expression for the immediate presence of God- 'a phrase to convey the idea of the most sublime blessedness.'

But, then we come to the crunch! In the next chapter, Paul writes, 'There was given to me a thorn in the flesh, a messenger of Satan to torment me.' God sent it, Satan used it.

A thorn in the flesh does not refer·to the general trials that we all experience but is an experience that can dominate our lives. We do not know what Paul's thorn was. Some scholars have suggested epilepsy, malaria, bad eye sight, depression or maybe it was his past when he persecuted the Christian church. We do not know, which is a good thing for if we knew then possibly most of us would be excluded. R.T. Kendall believes that most of us have a thorn. Another scholar writes, 'Is there a single servant of Christ who cannot point to some 'thorn in the flesh' visible or private, physical or psychological from which he has prayed to be released but which has been given to him by the Lord to keep him humble and therefore fruitful in His service.' Every believer must learn that human weakness and divine grace go hand in hand together.

If you have a thorn, you will certainly know what it is. R.T. Kendall lists loneliness, unhappy employment, unemployment, an enemy, a handicap, a sexual matter, an unhappy marriage, chronic illness, money matters, an unwanted calling.. ......He says the list is endless. Paul says his thorn was given to keep me from becoming conceited. F.F. Bruce says 'pride needs to be punctured'.

It is sad when people begin to take themselves seriously. Even Paul had to keep his feet on the ground. He says 'we have to remember that we need discipline. We need to be aware of our weakness.' He wrote to Timothy, 'Christ Jesus came into the world to save sinners, of whom I am the worst.' There are many paradoxes in the Christian faith and here is another - when we realise our own weakness, inadequacies, our own stupidity, sinfulness, then we can by God's grace be made strong and used for His glory.

Chapter 27
Palm Sunday

Palms are distinguished by their large compound evergreen leaves, known as fronds, arranged at the top of an unbranched stem. I'm afraid this reminds me of a joke: a chap wished to buy his mother some flowers for Mothers' Day. He visited a flower shop and asked for a bunch of anemones. The assistant apologised saying that they had sold out of anemones, but they had some palm leaves which were rather beautiful. On seeing them, he said they are gorgeous and declared with fronds like these who needs anemones.

Returning to palms, many produce products and food for human society there's the date palm, a concentrated energy food, coconut products, oils, palm syrup, wax, rattan cane, raffia, palm wood and, of course shelter all from palms. On Palm Sunday we will be looking at this well-known event once again. Finally, we should note that palms are symbols of victory and peace.

It is believed that Jesus visited Jerusalem on various occasions but this time things were going to be rather different. Jesus knew that He was approaching the end of His life on earth and He had made some special arrangements. He sent two of His disciples to collect a colt, a colt on which no one had ever sat on.

The disciples were challenged as they loosened the animal. 'What are you doing?' Their planned answer was 'The Lord needs it'. And they were allowed to bring the colt to Jesus. He sat on it and immediately the whole crowd of disciples burst into praises.

It was a carefully executed plan. The disciples were challenged and the answer met their password. 'The Lord needs it'. Over the last 2000 years, that statement would have been made thousands of times. Wouldn't it have been marvelous if the same act of sacrifice and obedience had been made by the disciples over these years. 'The Lord needs it.' Has that plea been made to us time and time again? What has been our response?

We often consider the failures of the Jewish nation in the Old Testament. Has the Christian Church in New Testament days been any better? When you consider it took the Church 1500 years to translate the Bible into a form of English that the plough boy could understand. When you consider it took 1800 years to pass a law against slavery.

But back to the story. The colt was presented to Jesus and He sat on it and great praises took off, but what has Jesus got in mind?

Let's remind ourselves of Jesus' situation. We read in John ch 11 v 57 'the Chief Priests and Pharisees had given orders that if anyone found out where Jesus was, he should report it so that they might arrest Him.' Jesus was a wanted man. The authorities wanted Him killed so why on earth did Jesus make these arrangements to draw attention to Himself by leading a procession followed by cheering crowds?

The answer is to found in Zechariah ch 9 v 9. 'Rejoice greatly, O Daughter of Zion! Shout, Daughter of Jerusalem! See, your King comes to you righteous and having salvation, gentle and riding on a donkey, on a colt, the foal of a donkey.' In those days, the donkey was not a lowly beast as we think today. The donkey was a noble beast and when a King or Conqueror entered a city on a donkey, it meant he came in peace. If he came on a horse, it was a symbol of war. Jesus came in love and peace and He still does to those who accept Him as Lord.

The Jews were a conquered people. Many were waiting for a leader who would drive out the Romans from their land. Do you remember way back when Jesus was presented by Mary and Joseph in the Temple? St. Luke ch 2 v 25-32. There was still the faithful few who knew the way of the Lord.

So what can we learn from Palm Sunday? There are four points we ought to note. 1. The gospel of Jesus is a gospel of love and peace. 2. It is a gospel that turns the values of the world upside down. 3. It is a gospel that demanded from Jesus a courage that the world had never seen before. This is the Son of God, the Creator of the Universe laying down His life in love and peace to save us from our sins. Surely, we ought to be more bold in our witness, to stand up for Jesus, to be counted, to identify with Our Saviour and finally, as far as the donkey was concerned 'The Lord needs it' and it was presented to the Lord. What does the Lord need from us? Our commitment, our love, our courage, our faithfulness. We must not be found wanting.

Chapter 28
Angels

Do you believe in angels?

If we accept the Scriptures, then of course we do and we are not alone. According to a recent Gallup poll in the U.S.A., 72% of the population believe in angels, half of whom believe they have felt an angel's presence. Throughout America, there is a wave of new interest in angels (or angelology!).

In one year, a few years ago, 115 new books came to the market on the subject, there were 3 glossy magazines and hundreds of shops which sold angel paraphernalia.

There is also evidence that the subject is attracting interest in the U.K. We have had one or two T.V. programmes recently and books are appearing in the shops with various angel themes in particular personal accounts of people who claim to have seen angels.

Why do so many people now believe in angels? One lady replied, "This is a very fearful world that we live in. People need assurance that God really cares. Sending us angels is one of the ways that God responds to our needs." Another said," People thought they would have a job tor life, a marriage for life, but now they're finding these things are not eternal. So they start looking for something to hold on to, when they are sinking - and you can always hold on to the angel's wonderful wings."

Polly Toynbee in the Christmas issue of the Radio Times takes a different view. She says "If we each have a

121

guardian angel where are they when you need them?......If people's gods or hosts of angels are so good, why don't they intervene more often? If they can do miracles sometimes at random for a few ordinary people, why not for every deserving case all the time........ "

What then are the implications of a belief in angels? Is it "believe and all will be well"?

This is certainly not the Christian gospel. The gospel is a gospel of forgiveness through the sacrifice of the Lord Jesus. It is a gospel of challenge and of commitment. Nowhere does Jesus promise us a life without problems, suffering or sacrifice. But in it all, He does promise us His presence, grace and power. Do we need to ask for anything more?

Do we serve Him in order to gain an easy life or for what we are going to receive in due time - i.e., eternal life?

There are then different ways in which we can believe in angels. Let us acknowledge them as God's helpers and our co-workers in the great task of spreading the Good News of Jesus Christ.

Chapter 29
The Reformation

Up to the 14th Century the Roman Catholic church had all the might and power. Everything was controlled by the church. Services were held in Latin which the common people were unable to understand. They just had to do as they were told. There was confession, penances and indulgences. To do right was a matter of confession where penances and indulgences were given out in order to avoid suffering in purgatory - a place of suffering for sins in order to be good enough to enter Heaven.

This form of rule over the people is not in accord with Holy Scripture. In fact, the place of Scripture was difficult to locate! I found a quotation from, I believe, a Scottish Bishop who said, 'I thank God that I never knew quite what the Old and New Testaments were.' Over many years, the church moved away from Holy Scripture.

During the 14th Century and, no doubt, before, many good men began to question the position of the church. As stated all worship was in Latin. The common people had no clue what the truth was.

John Wyclif started writing in English and with help began an English translation of the Vulgate, being the Latin edition of the Bible in around 1380. He also wrote pamphlets on various subjects and suggested the church would be better without a pope! We can imagine how his work was viewed by the authorities. His followers were arrested and forced to recant.

This reformed movement was not only in England. The first German Bible was published in 1466, an Italian Bible was published in 1471 and a French one in around 1500. The sources used were the Latin Vulgate, the Hebrew edition and a Greek version translated by Erasmus a colleague of Martin Luther.

The R.C. church declared that the publication of the Bible in the language of the people disobeyed the church.

John Wyclif avoided arrest and died in 1384 but in 1428 his bones were dug up, burned and cast into the River Swift. But the movement carried on. William Tyndale, a brilliant translator, came on to the scene. He was determined to produce another English translation - his theme was all authority is founded on God's grace. He sought permission to translate the Bible into English, but was refused and had to flee to Germany where he met Martin Luther. Later Tyndale actually produced a copy of his work for Anne Boleyn but was later betrayed and arrested in Antwerp where he was strangled and burned in 1536.

One great advantage the translators had over previous ones was that printing was now available (around the 1470s) which greatly assisted in the dissemination of the Word.

Martin Luther was born in 1483. He took a degree but was interested in theology and studied for 3 years in a monastery. He became a priest and went to preach and lecture at the University of Wittenberg. He was a professor of theology, composer, priest and monk. On a mission to Rome, Martin Luther was appalled by the corrupt practices in particular the sale of indulgences to raise money for building purposes. The Rome experience turned Luther into a reformer.

He began to preach salvation by faith not by works and in 1517 drew up a list of *95* theses on indulgences and nailed them to the door of the church. Thus started the reformation. We could say that Luther was a catalyst of all that was brewing up in Europe.

Chapter 30
Heaven and Hell

(Scripture and thoughts....) ·

I have just read a book entitled 'IS HELL FOR REAL OR DOES EVERYONE GO TO HEAVEN?' It was written by half a dozen American evangelists. They all seem to agree that NOT everyone will go to Heaven and that the only way to get to Heaven is to accept Jesus Christ as a personal Saviour in this life. I have also read bits of another book 'What Christians believe' by David Craig who quotes many Christian teachers who maintain that it may not be as clear cut as it seems.

Now, of course, most Christians believe that Jesus is the way, the truth and the life and that no one comes to the Father except through Him. (St John ch 14 v 6) and 'Salvation is found in no one else.' (Acts ch 4 v 12).

When I have been asked in the past 'How will those who have never heard of Jesus get on on Judgement Day (e.g. some South American tribes)? I have always maintained that my God Who is a God of Love will surely judge them according to the light that they have received. (see St. John ch 1 v 9 The true light that gives light to *every* man.). Come to think of it, if they have not heard of Jesus then it is our fault anyway (or the fault of the Christian Church). But why just South American tribes, what about the tribes in England who may never have heard a clear exposition of the Christian gospel? Again, aren't we to blame?

(There are some Christians who still say that those South American tribes would be eternally lost and who almost seem to be proud of the stand that they take).

There are some people who have closed their ears, minds and hearts to the Gospel because of the hideous way that they have been treated by so-called Christians. We all know that the Christian Church has much to answer for. How careful we, who believe, have to be in all our dealings with others, believers and non-believers alike.

Joel Edwards says that we have to accept Jesus as Saviour in *this* life. Those of us who have accepted Jesus in this life rejoice in that blessed relationship but hold on! I have had over 80 years to find the Saviour. How many years are we given to make up our minds? Suppose a young lad dies at 11 years old or 16 or 21 years. At what point would he be considered accountable and responsible for any decisions? Should there not be a level playing field? But, it isn't just age, all the circumstances of life should be considered as with the South American tribes.

Another thought: How could anyone enjoy Heaven if they knew a relative or friend just had not made it? (Revelation ch 21 v 4) 'He will wipe every tear from their eyes. There will be no more death or mourning or crying or pain, for the old order of things has passed away.'

One of the American writers (Robert W. Yarbrough) criticises John Stott for saying 'I find the concept (of eternal conscious torment) intolerable and do not understand how people can live with it without cauterising their feelings or cracking under the strain.' Yarbrough continues 'With Stott I affirm that eternal conscious punishment strains our sense of justice. It weighs heavily on our emotions. But so does the daily news.' How on earth can he compare eternal conscious punishment with the daily news no matter how tragic?

A second American writer (R. Albert Mohler) also criticises John Stott who maintains that the church has misunderstood some key biblical texts. In St Matthew ch 10 v 28 for instance, Stott says that the word for destroy meant complete destruction rather than everlasting punishment. Stott also states that in Revelation ch 20 v 14 the 'lake of fire' was not intended to suggest eternal torment for unbelieving humans. He says 'Would there not (otherwise)..... be a serious disproportion between sins consciously committed in time and torment consciously experienced throughout eternity?' John Stott then appears to accept an annihilationist view of hell fire i.e. if someone is sent to hell they are destroyed.

William Barclay tells us that the word Gehenna is regularly translated as hell and is a form of the word Hinnom, a word with an evil history. It is a ravine outside of Jerusalem where Ahaz, King of Judah, sacrificed children including his son in heathen worship. Josiah declared Hinnom unclean and it became the place where the Jerusalem rubbish was burnt. It soon represented a symbol of hell where the souls of the wicked will be tortured and destroyed.

I definitely believe in the Final Judgement for all, believers and non-believers alike. Here are some scripture references: St. Matthew ch 16 v 27, Acts ch 10 v 42, Romans ch 14 v 10-12 and 2 Corinthians ch 5 v 10.

What will happen at the Final Judgement? Who knows? I rejoice in the fact that God knows and we can trust God Our Father and the Lord Jesus Christ. As Abraham said, 'Will not the Judge of all the earth do right?' For believers we have Romans ch 8 v 1: 'Therefore, there is no condemnation for those who are in Christ Jesus.' But, it seems that since our conversion, we will still have to give an account of our living. As David Craig says 'It is not a question of earning our salvation by good works but works are the evidence of the reality of our faith through which believers are saved.' It does appear that at the Final Judgement there will be a separation of the sheep and goats, but what then?

What are we to make of these verses? 'Consequently, just as the result of one trespass was condemnation for all men, so also the result of one act of righteousness was justification that brings life for *all* men' (Romans ch 5 v 18) and 'For God has bound all men over to disobedience so that He may have mercy on them *all.* , (Romans ch 11 v 32). 'For as in Adam all die, so in Christ *all* will be made alive.' (1 Corinthians ch 15 v 22). 'that at the name of Jesus *every* knee should bow, in heaven and on earth and under the earth and *every* tongue confess that Jesus Christ is Lord to the Glory of God the Father. (Philippians ch 2 v 10,11). 'The Lord is not slow in keeping His promise, as some understand slowness. He is patient with you, not wanting anyone to perish, but everyone to come to repentance.' (2 Peter ch 3 v 9).

I do believe in hell, a place reserved for the devil and his angels. Many years ago, I read a book by F.W.Farrar, in which he recorded a vision of an angel with outstretched arms. In one hand he held a cup of water and in the other he had a curtain. He said he was going to quench hell and hide Heaven in order that men might learn to love God just for what He was. And, a last word from William Barclay: ' ...for the Christian the matter is even more compelling, for our fear is not that God will punish us, but our fear is that we may grieve His love.'

Chapter 31
Athanasius

Atbanasius 297 - 373 (**Athanasius was an opponent of Arius – the Arians – who would not accept Jesus as part of the Godhead**)

Athanasius was a Greek of Alexandra. As a young boy, he came to the attention of Alexander, Bishop of Alexandria, who took him into his home. He gave him a good education and introduced him to the best thinkers of that day. He was most studious and his main interest was the doctrine of salvation about which he wrote (De Incamatione) before celebrating his 21st birthday, so it is not surprising to see him as a leading opponent of Arius at the Council of Nicaea where he made a great impression and where Arianism was excluded. Athanasius' theme: 'Its main position is that the Logos must be truly God or we cannot be saved',

Athanasius had a great friend in Eustathius Bishop of Antioch, who had been a strong opponent of Origen who himself had been supported by Lucian and Eusebius of Caesarea. As time passed by after the Council of Nicaea, the Arians sought to find a way back. There were doubts existing around the Council. Had the Council been too quick in its decision making? Had the discussions been wide enough? Had there been too much pressure from outside (i.e. the Emperor)?

These doubts and a relaxation in attitudes led to an amnesty in 327 for those who had been exiled. This seemed to give the returning exiles an opportunity for 'pay back' time. They felt that it was, perhaps, too early to attack the Council and Creed so their vitriol was aimed at Atbanasius' friends.

Eustatbius was the first to suffer an attack which was not aimed at his doctrinal position but at his alleged immorality. This failed. Eustatbius was a staunch opponent of Lucian whilst Helena, the Emperor's mother, was a keen supporter. This provided a sensitive situation into which poor Eustathius fell completely, and, as a result, was deposed and exiled. Other friends were also attacked, then it became the tum of Athanasius. In 326, he became Bishop of Alexandria. He was still young and impetuous and perhaps used his authority to deal with the Meletians too harshly. (Bishop Meletius was an associate of Arius).

From then on, it seemed that Athanasius' position depended on who was the current Emperor. The Arians and the Meletians accused Athanasius of interfering with the grain supplies from Egypt and Constantine exiled him without any formal trial. There were also various false charges including murder. But when Constantine died in 337, Athanasius was able to return to Alexandria only to be exiled a year later by Constantius. Athansius took refuge in Rome where Constans was Emperor and in 346, through the Emperor, Athanasius returned triumphantly to Egypt. Constans died in 350 and Constantius became sole Emperor, renewing his pro-Arian policy, and Athanasius was banished again! Constantius died in 361 and Athanasius returned once more. He convened a Council in 362 and pursued church unity. but on the arrival of Emperor Vanens in 365, another pro-Arian, his exile was reinstated but a little later this was eased and Athanasius was able to spend a few years peacefully at home before his death in 373. Thankfully. all these comings and goings did not restrict his tremendous output of writing on behalf of the Gospel.

Chapter 32
Paul goes to Rome

PAUL'S LAST JOURNEY - TO ROME

At the conclusion of chapter 26 of Acts, King Agrippa says to Festus, the Roman Governor, 'This man (Paul) could have been set free if he had not appealed to Caesar'. Previously in Jerusalem, Paul had been arrested, mainly for his own protection. Many Jews were intent on killing him, in fact over forty had taken an oath not to eat or drink anything until they had indeed killed him. The Roman authorities had stepped in (because Paul was a Roman citizen) and had moved him to Caeserea, the seat of Roman government, to keep him away from the Jewish crowds.

The next move now was to send Paul to Rome. In Acts chapter 27, we come across once again a 'we' passage meaning, of course, that Luke was accompanying Paul and giving us a first-hand account of all that was happening. Paul also has another companion, Aristarchus (referred to in Colossians chapter 4 verse ten as a fellow prisoner i.e. in Rome with Paul).

Both John Stott and William Barclay suggest that the only way Paul's two companions could travel with him to Rome was by being recognised as Paul's slaves. Supreme loyalty on their part.

The three men were handed over to Julius, a centurion who belonged to the Imperial Regiment and they boarded ship. The first stop was a little way up the coast to Sidon, where Julius shows kindness in allowing Paul to meet with some disciples for a brief farewell. They sail on northwards to Cyprus and because of strong westerly winds they pass under the lee of the island sailing north. Paul would have been very familiar with this area. His home was in Tarsus, just a few miles north and his first missionary journey was around this area. The ship continues sailing west to Myra where they change ships for another from Alexandria in Egypt which was carrying grain to Rome. They continue sailing between the mainland and the island of Rhodes aiming for Cnidus but a strong wind forces the ship south towards Crete. They hug the coast and arrive at Fair Havens south of the island. They now face a dilemma. It is evident that conditions are getting worse.

Paul was a very experienced traveller. One scholar has calculated that Paul up to now had travelled 3,500 miles by sea and he offers the company the advice that it would be unwise to continue at this time and would be safer to stay in Fair Havens until the weather improves. The pilot, the ship owner and the centurion all disagree on account of Fair Havens being unsuitable for a stay and they decide to continue and head for Phoenix about another 40 miles.

So, they set sail. As soon as they do a wind of hurricane force sweeps down from the Cretan mountains and blows the ship into open sea - south. They were supposed to be going northwest to Rome. They pass by an island called Cauda and another danger appears. They are not far from the North African coast where the Syrtis sands threaten. They have been called the Goodwin Sands of the Mediterranean.

The crew start to take precautions. They manage to haul the lifeboat on board, they begin to 'frapp' the ship i.e. they pass cables round the ship to hold it together, they jettison some of the cargo and what tackle and equipment that could be spared and finally they give up all hope of being saved!

Now, it is Paul's time. He reminds them that he had been proved right earlier. He was not in the mind to make cheap points but he now wanted them to listen. He urges them to take courage and he assures them that no one will be lost. 'My God has assured me that all will be saved, Only the ship will be lost.' They battle on and eventually the sailors sense that they are approaching land. They take soundings, 120 feet, 90 feet. The sailors see a chance to escape the nightmare journey, but Paul warns the centurion that everyone must stay for all to be saved and the soldiers cut the ropes of the lifeboat which falls away.

Paul was a man with both feet firmly planted. The company had not been able to eat for fourteen days. 'You must take food. You need it to survive.' He gives thanks and they eat, all 276 of the company. John Stott writes, 'Paul was an integrated Christian who combined spirituality with sanity and faith and works.'

Daylight comes, they do not know where they are, but decide to run the ship aground. The ship strikes a sandbar and begins to break up. Yet another danger appears. The soldiers prepare to kill the prisoners. If a

Roman soldier loses a prisoner then he must bear the punishment of the prisoner. The centurion intervenes in order to save Paul and tells everyone to try to save themselves which they do.

The island on which they land is Malta where they find much kindness and stay for three months until a ship is available to take them on to Rome. In fact, they later arrive at Puteoli, the port for Rome which is about forty miles from the city. This, by the way, is the third time Paul had been shipwrecked! (See 2 Corinthians chapter 11 v 22-33).

* * *

Paul had spread the gospel throughout Palestine, Syria, Turkey and Greece using modern names and as he writes in Romans chapter 15 verses 23-29, his vision was to go to Spain and visit the Romans on the way. He was a Roman citizen, free born, and he longed to see Rome, even more so as the Apostle to the Gentiles.

The Roman Empire has been described as 'the grandest political achievement ever accomplished'. It most certainly helped with the spread of the Gospel. The Empire was 'efficient in administration and postal communications and it facilitated travel by its ambitious system of roads and ports, policed by its legions and its navy, so preserving for the benefit of all long-standing *pax romana'* (John Stott). Pax romana refers to the period from 27 BC to 180 AD when throughout the known world there was relative peace. The odd skirmish, of course, occurred e.g. in Britain but generally there was world peace.

Paul's heart must have throbbed with great excitement as he was about to enter the capital of the world. 'He saw warships in the distance, nearby were the beaches of Baiae which was the Brighton of Italy....the coloured sails of the yachts of the wealthy Romans. Puteoli, Rome's port, with its wharves and store-houses has been called the Liverpool of the ancient world' (William Barclay). Of course, there was another side to the splendour of Rome. Seneca called it ' a cesspool of iniquity' and Romans chapter one, Paul himself refers to its moral decadence.

As the group began their journey from Puteoli to the centre of Rome, another surprise faced them. A deputation of brother Christians had walked from Rome, about 40 miles, to welcome them. Paul had never been to Rome. When he wrote his letter to them - a remarkable statement of the Christian Faith - he was writing to a vibrant church, so just a thought - how was the Gospel spread to Rome?? It was spread by the faith and love of ordinary men and women striving, to live for the Lord Jesus Christ. This is the way the Salvation Army was mainly spread. It was not through directives from the Army's headquarters, though this did happen occasionally, but ordinary men and women moved around taking the Gospel with them. Later, they would ask the Army to send officers to establish the work which had been started.

If you were the only Christian where you live, what would you do? I find this a challenging thought. Our situation is certainly not like Paul's. Who was the Emperor when he arrived in Rome? Nero! Paul arrived a prisoner of Rome and it *is* believed he died a few years

141

later at the hands of Nero, but not before, he had contacted many people and written wonderful letters to the Ephesians, Philippians, Colossians etc.

We are not alone, like Paul, we have the unseen cloud of witnesses around us, we have the knowledge that we belong to a worldwide fellowship, we know that wherever we go, there is God and we know that the Risen Saviour by the power of the Holy Spirit is with us and within us. May the Lord help us to be as faithful, courageous. daring and loving as His servant Paul_

Chapter 33
Daily Bread

GIVE US THIS DAY OUR DAILY BREAD

Bible Readings: St Matt ch 6 v 5 – 15

Exodus ch 16 v 1 – 36

St John ch 6 v 27 - 35

When we pray the Lord's Prayer, we begin by being absorbed by great and lofty thoughts about God, where He is, His Name, His Kingdom and His will. We almost forget ourselves, which is no bad thing! But, then Jesus brings us right down to earth. 'Give us this day our daily bread. ' A prayer for our physical needs.

Jesus knows all too well, that we are body and spirit. We have spiritual needs and bodily needs - both have to be met.

Too many neglect their spiritual needs. I wonder what percentage will go to church next Sunday or how many will walk in the country and become part of nature, acknowledging their dependence on the Lord.

I think that it is amazing that people wonder why crime is rife, why there is so much misery, why there is so much dependence on drugs and drink, why moral standards are slipping to lower and lower levels when all the time their spiritual needs are being ignored. We must get back to the Bible. Living with Jesus is no miserable experience. It is life fulfilling. It is soul satisfying. Yes, I'm afraid many neglect their spiritual needs.

There are those who neglect their physical needs. Anorexia nervosa is a terrible illness. To see young girls literally fading away. The problem is that loved ones don't know how to cope and to deal with the illness. We see models in fashion shows on TV so very thin and, of course, there are sham forms of religion that neglect bodily needs.

F.W. Farrar suggests that were we to pray only this petition, our prayers would be as material as the howling of a young lion. On the other hand, if this petition was omitted, then our prayers might become fantastic, impractical, the prayers of dreamers.

We are body and spirit. We have prayed for the spirit and now Jesus teaches us how to pray for the body. We can learn much from this petition.

GIVE US. A prayer of absolute dependence on God. We realise our need and reliance on Him. There was an advert where a little boy cries FEED ME. It's much the same. GIVE US.

Someone said, 'Worldly men are like swine which plunder the acorns but do not look up to the oak from which they fall.

Do we acknowledge the One who gives and gives and gives again? Have we forgotten the practice of saying Grace? Jesus gave thanks. A humble meal, any meal, can be a Holy Communion. The Founder suggested that 'Grace before meat' can be a sacrament. Let us remember to thank the Lord who provides all good things.

The Lord's prayer starts 'Our Father' reminding us of the Family of God's people. This petition continues GIVE US again reinforcing this theme. God's people all round the world, whatever creed, colour, state. Jesus in this phrase rebukes our selfishness.

GIVE US THIS DAY - sufficient for the day. St Matt ch 6 v 34 'Therefore do not worry about tomorrow, for tomorrow will worry about itself. Each day has enough trouble of its own.' In the reading about the Children of Israel, we read 'The people are to go out each day and gather enough for that day.' Jesus wants us to be free from worry and care. Trust Him for to-day. Be free from the fever of building up around ourselves a freak sense of security. Be free from things.

St. Luke ch 12 v 13 - 21. The rich fool.

Give us this day - not worrying about the future, not living in the past, but living truly and nobly a day at a time.

A teacher once told his students to repent the day before they die. 'Does a man know the day of his death?' The answer 'Let a man repent to-day lest he should die tomorrow. So, will his life be one of repentance.' That sounds grim, but it need not be. Living daily in the presence of Christ, in His forgiveness, in His Love, in His strength and in His Joy.

145

GIVE US THIS DAY OUR DAILY BREAD. Our daily bread - that which is due to us through our payment of diligent work. Barrow said, 'Give us our daily bread, we pray even in that one little word that we may live lives of happy industry and honest aim'.

Paul was severe with the Thessalonians 2 ch 3 v 10 'For even when we were with you, we gave you this rule "If a man will not work, he shall not eat"'.

DAILY BREAD - that which we need to maintain our lives. Jesus would teach us the folly of imagining that there is happiness in having much. This prayer safeguards our physical needs but it also goes deeper for we know Jesus is the Bread of Life.

St. John ch 6 v 27 - 35.

Let us pray this prayer in thankfulness and in complete reliance and trust in the Lord Jesus Christ.

Chapter 34
Holy Bible

A little boy found a Bible in a cupboard at home. He asked his mother, 'Whose is this book?' She replied, 'It's a Bible. It's God's book.' He answered, 'Don't you think we ought to send it back to him? We never read it.'

I wonder if we sometimes take the Bible for granted. We often forget the lives which have been sacrificed in order that we might have this book. We often forget the sheer hard work of translation which has brought the Bible to us. We often forget the learning which has been necessary e.g. the N.I.V.

Now, we are very fortunate because we speak English and there are very many different translations that are available to us to give us light and understanding, but supposing there was not a translation in our language.

The Bible Society has a Bible a Month Club which helps to raise money for Bible translations for all over the world. It also suggests prayer themes and members are asked to remember the translators working on various projects.

These figures may be a little dated but recently in Africa there were 2000 languages but only 624 had some part of the Scriptures, 227 had a portion, 259 had a New Testament and only 138 had the whole Bible. This left over 60% with nothing.

In Tanzania, an old woman, on hearing the New Testament being read in her language was amazed. She said, 'Is Christianity also for my people? I thought it was only for those who spoke Swahili.

At a leprosy hospital in Madagascar, a patient thanked the Bible Society for providing a portion of Scripture in his own language. He said 'I came to know that Jesus loves people like us and I gave my heart to Him.'

There was uproar in Nigeria when it was announced that copies of the Scriptures would not be on sale until a later date. One man offered to leave his motor bike as security to ensure he received a copy.

When a Bible was published in the local language in Zaire, a pastor was overjoyed and said, 'Now we have the Bible in our language, God speaks clearly and directly to our hearts, and we understand His message for our lives to-day. We are grateful to the Bible Society and all its supporters for making it possible for us to have God's Word. It is like Christ Himself has come to visit us....

Let us treasure God's Word and read it regularly.

Chapter 35
Pentecost

Pentecost is when: we celebrate the coming of the Holy Spirit and which is also the birth of the Christian Church.

Some churches and Sunday Schools have birthday cakes at Pentecost. And, why not, it is our birthday.

Why was the church born at Pentecost? Because it was at Pentecost that God sent His Spirit, baptizing the disciples with power, enabling them to declare boldly the truths about Jesus.

It was a rowdy affair. Some people thought the disciples were drunk and Peter had to explain: Acts ch 2. The next Sunday is Trinity Sunday, when we think of God the Father, God the Son and God the Holy Spirit - a mystery that it is hard for us to understand.

Most of us find it relatively easy to relate to God the Father Our Father in Heaven, the Creator, Preserver and Governor of all men and things. Sceptics would pull our legs about the old gentleman above with His flowing white beard looking down on us all. We find it perhaps easier to relate to Jesus Christ, the Son of God who lived in Palestine 2000 years ago. We can read the wonderful stories about Him. We can see the many paintings conjured up in the imaginations of countless artists. At Christmas we celebrate His birth. At Easter we remembered His dying and glorious resurrection. Yes, we can relate to Him.

But, the Holy Spirit? There's nothing there to see. We cannot imagine a spirit or wind. Mind you, we can feel the presence of the wind - something to think about.

Can we use our imaginations? Let us go back to the times when Jesus was here. We hear enough about time travel. We will attach ourselves to the group of disciples. Everyday, we lap up the unbelievable things which are happening. We see the blind receive their sight, the deaf hear, the lame walk, the hungry are fed, it goes on day after day. Every night, we hardly sleep, the events of the day go through our minds, we live again the scenes we have witnessed. We awake anticipating another fantastic day. Now and then, Jesus takes us aside and talks to us. With all the excitement, it is hard to take it all in. He teaches us about His Father and how we should love each other, and then one day, right out of the blue, He says, 'It is for your good that I am going away.'

How shocked we would have been. Utterly astounded. What on earth is He talking about? How can it possibly be for our good if He goes away? He talks about sorrow and suffering. Why is all this coming to an end? We have known joy, peace, comfort, security, purpose.

We have known His power, seen His miracles - now, is it all coming to an end?

The disciples were just like us - slow to learn. How could Jesus remain with them always?

We sing sometimes, 'I wish that His hands had been placed on my head, that His arm had been thrown around me, and that I might have seen His kind look when He said: Let the little ones come unto me!' We forget that if He was with us or with me, He would not be able to be with anyone else.

Jesus must have felt so restricted in a human body. Confined to one place and any one time. Can we imagine Jesus with us in physical form here to-day? What a day we would have, but what about to-morrow? We would all want Him to accompany us to our own particular activity. The children would want to take Him to school, the adults would want to take Him to the workplace or home. There would be some arguments.

We forget what Peter said about Jesus in Acts ch 2 v 38 'Repent and be baptized, every one of you, in the name of Jesus Christ for the forgiveness of your sins. And you will receive the gift of the Holy Spirit. The promise is for you.... ' And Jesus said in St John ch 16 v 7' ..It is for your good that I am going away. Unless I go away, the Counsellor will not come to you; but if I go, I will send Him to you.'

The presence of Jesus by the Holy Spirit is as real as any physical presence and we can all know His presence every day of our lives. Didn't Jesus say 'Lo. I am with you always, even unto the end of the world.'

My father had as a second Christian name, the name 'Emmanuel' perhaps at times an embarrassment, but what a reminder 'God with US'

So, there is no need for any arguments. We can all take the Lord Jesus, by His Spirit, with us tomorrow wherever we go. The children can take Him to school.

You can take Him to work. You can keep Him at home with you. But, for a moment, let us turn this truth around.

Have you ever been ignored? Have you entered a cafe on your own for a meal and waited and waited? You wonder if you have suddenly become invisible..... Or maybe, you've joined a group of friends and nobody spoke to *you*. Like the chap who went to the doctor. He explained that he felt he had become invisible and the doctor said 'Next '.

I wonder how often the Holy Spirit has felt like that? We ask Him along, then in the midst of life we fret and care, we panic, feel inadequate, and all the time if only we paid attention to Him, He would guide us and empower us. We fail under the burden of the day when all the time we have the resources of God at our disposal... they remain ignored, neglected.

How foolish to ask for light in a dark room when all we need to do is switch on the light. How stupid to feel cold by an unlit fire, how ridiculous to cry 'I'm thirsty' when we could turn on the tap. Yet every day, we all neglect the resources of God when He desires to do so much for us.

Whatever our need, it can be met by the Holy Spirit. I didn't say, it will be met, it can be met, but we must allow Him to come. Let us all empty our hands of the mediocre which surrounds us and fully accept Our Lord and Saviour Jesus Christ by the power of the Holy Spirit.

Chapter 36
St. Augustine

Augustine Saint, Bishop and Christian.Philosopher.

Augustine was born in Tagaste (Numidia). North Africa, in 354. He was the son of a pagan, Patricius, who was converted late in life, and Monica, regardcd as a saintly mother. He spent 14 years in Carthage leaming rhetoric and during this time had an illegitimate son in 372.- Augustine was 18 years old. He turned to more serious study and followed the Manicheans, a mixture of old Babylonian religion, Zoroastrianism, Gnosticism and Christianity but he became disillusioned when he met their leader. He was invited to take up a teaching post in Milan by which time he had become a complete sceptic, but then he met Ambrose. His own record of his conversion is deeply moving with many tears and much struggling but Augustine finds peace in Paul's letter to the Romans ch 13. Augustine was 32 years old. He was ordained a priest in 391 and four years later was consecrated Coadjutor-Bishop of Hippo. He succeeded to the diocese in 396. ·

Augustine as Bishop had initially problems with the Donatists and much of his early writings were of a controversial nature, but then he set about writing such classics as his 'Confessions' 'one of the most popular books of all time' which is autobiographical but using the tool of psychology, and 'City of God' which took him about 14 years to write. This book was a reply to the idea that the fall of Rome was due to embracing Christianity. Augustine showed how world events reflect the purposes and judgements of God.·

Augustine did not enjoy good health and his huge output of writings was made possible by a team of stenographers. We have 400 sermons, over 200 letters, Scriptural commentaries and homilies as evidence of his output. Much of his writing was in response to appeals for help with various problems and revealed tireless effort to combat controversy. His theology was set out in 'De Trinitate' and 'De Doctrina Christiana'. 'The Holy Spirit is believed to proceed from the Son as well as from the Father, and the threefold relation is that of lover, the beloved and the love that flows between them.'·

One example of Augustine's opponents was Pelagius, thought to be Irish, who came to Rome around 400 and was disturbed by the low state of morals. He also found it difficult to accept some of Augustine's writings. Pelagius seemed to have a great faith in man's ability to help himself. He denied the concept of original sin and seemed also to give little credence to the idea of redemption. This contrasted with Augustine's belief that 'man in his natural condition since the fall of Adam is thoroughly depraved'. Augustine's doctrine of grace and predestination began a controversy which has continued down the ages. There have been groups referred to as Pelagians, semi-Pelagians, Semi-Augustinians and Augustinians. Today, we have the 'Reformed' view headed by Augustine and including Martin Luther and John Calvin and the 'Opposing' views whose proponents include John Wesley, Charles Finney and coming up-to-date Billy Graham. There's no doubt the controversy will run on!

Augustine died in 430 'the major Christian theologian of the early Christian Church'.

Chapter 37
Discrimination

The basis of my opinion:

I have friends who are 'gay' - a word incidentally which I do not understand though I know what it now means and am sad at the change in meaning from the delight it had in earlier days. The fact that they are 'gay' makes no difference at all to our relationship. I respect them, treat them like any other friends who do not share their nomenclature, but I do not wish to know anything about the 'gay' side of their lives. The reason for this is that I have grave doubts about homosexuality.

If people have a genuine propensity to homosexuality, I feel sorry for them. I do not understand why there should be such an orientation but I believe it is unnatural and wrong to give in to such a tendency and to practice such sexuality. There are many such men who have risen above this pressure.

During Question Tune recently a discussion arose about discrimination and one speaker said that it is wrong to practice discrimination against colour, creed and sexuality. No right minded person would argue with this. To take advantage of gays and lesbians in any way is totally unacceptable. They should be loved and cared for and, if possible, understood, never ill-treated or bullied. But, I do have a reservation about classing those three groups (i.e. colour, creed and sexuality) together. Let me explain. We are all coloured! Colour should make no difference at all. We are all God's children. As for creed, we are simply asked to love others regardless.

Some people might say that they have an orientation towards paedophilia. Should we discriminate against them? We should certainly not allow them to practice this perversion.

When I was about 14 years old, an older Christian friend invited me to stay with him. We slept in the same bed. I had been brought by Christian parents and had not the slightest clue about life particularly anything sexual - a truly sheltered upbringing. But, when he made advances, I knew instinctively that it was wrong. Over 70 years later that opinion is stronger than ever.

I thank God for the sexual orientation which I have. When God made women, He knew what He was doing! I thank God for a lovely wife. We have a blessed relationship and we are both in love and faithful. I heard a man once say that since getting married, he had never looked at another woman. I cannot say that. I often see women whom I regard as beautiful and I appreciate their beauty but it does not mean that because I have a particular orientation, I should be able to embrace them. After all, external beauty, we know, is only skin deep. And, there must be discipline in life. There must be faithfulness and devotion to one's partner. As stated, my wife and I love and care for each other. I would not have it any other way. The rewards for such a relationship are countless.

In this statement, I have not referred to the Bible. Our conduct is clearly shown in that wonderful hook. For example: Read Paul's letter to the Romans chapter one.

Chapter 38
Three Wise Men

St. Matthew ch 2 v 1-12/13-18

The visit of the three wise men is a story 2000 years old. You have heard it many times before, however let us look at it once again.

How many wise men were there? We assume three, but there could have many more. The Bible does not say how many, we assume three because there were three gifts, but can you imagine one or two of them could have been like us. Oh, I forgot my present!

They came from the east. Herodotus, a Greek historian of the 5th century says they were Medes (from Media, present day Azerbaijan) which was part of the Persian empire. The Medes had failed in trying to overthrow the Persians and so the Medes became a tribe of priests, holy and wise Magi, like with the Children of Israel, the Levites were the priestly tribe. They must have studied Hebrew Scripture e.g. Numbers ch 24 v 17 'A star will come out of Jacob, a sceptre will rise out of Israel.' And in particular from Micah ch 5 v 2. Read.

Again, the Bible does not give their names but tradition calls them Caspar, Balthazar and Melchior. I think we have to be a bit careful and need to make a distinction between Scripture truth and tradition. There are thousands of prophecies in the Old Testament which have been and are being fulfilled, and there are thousands of stories from traditions which have been handed down from generation to generation which are interesting but that's as far as they go.

In those days, most people believed in astrology. Normally the stars behave in regular and unvarying courses, but if a star suddenly glows with an unusual brilliance, it appeared that God was trying to tell men something special like the coming of a king. In conjunction with this, there was the expectation that Roman historians felt that something was going to happen. Suetonius, a Roman historian, tell us that Augustus, the Emperor, was being hailed as the Saviour of the world. There was expectation.

A word about Herod - Herod the Great. Herod became Governor in 47 BC. In 40 BC he was crowned King and he reigned till 4 BC. Initially, he did much good. He was a great builder, he built the Temple in Jerusalem. He could be generous especially during a famine in 25 BC, but as he got older he became insanely suspicious and his cruelty became known throughout the world. I will not record the terrible things he did, but Augustus said it was safer to be one of his pigs than one of his sons. When he reached 70 years, he thought he was going to die and he made terrible provision, involving suffering for many people to be carried out in the event of his death. St Matthew ch 2 Verse 3 ......

Back to the three wise men. When did they actually visit Jesus and worship Him? We do not know. It could have been almost straightaway, but it could also have been some months after Jesus' birth. Verse 11, 'On coming to the house, they saw the child with His mother Mary and they bowed down and worshipped Him.' They came into a house. It is thought that there had been some delay, because when Herod found that he had been outwitted by the wise men, in his mad rage he slaughtered all the boys in Bethlehem who were two years old or younger. So, we do not know. What we do know is that they bowed down and worshipped Jesus. It is said that years ago wise men worshipped Jesus. Today, wise men still do.

Not only did they worship Jesus, but they presented gifts. I am going to be frivolous now! Supposing instead of three wise men, they had been three wise women! What would they have brought? Diane, my wife, suggests a bundle of linen, salt and oil. I think maybe a casserole or a blanket.....

Gold: a gift for a King. Some suggest that they were Kings based on verses in Isaiah and Psalm 72.
Frankincense: a gift for a Deity for offering prayer.
Myrrh: an embalming ointment signifying suffering and death.

It would be interesting to know where the inspiration came from for these gifts. It was probably the Hebrew scriptures. We know full well the prophesies about Jesus' life, suffering and death, and glorious resurrection.

Chapter 39
Jonah

At the end of the Old Testament, there is a collection of what are called 12 minor prophets. They appear after Daniel and start with Hosea. They are not in chronological order but all have something to offer to the Word of God. There are gems in all of them and, of course, wonderful prophesies. Jonah is the fifth minor prophet and his book is unique. While the rest contain prophesies, Jonah's contains a story and we all know what that story is.

Sorry about this, but I'm going to remind you again about the story and perhaps a few bits of information you may have missed.

We meet Jonah first of all in 2 Kings ch 14 v 25. He follows two of Israel's most famous prophets, Elijah and Elisha, and has a similar task. Elijah was called to preach to Sidon, Elisha was called to preach to Syria and Jonah was called to preach to Nineveh. So what you say? These countries were not Jewish, they were heathen or gentile. Nineveh was a very important city in Assyria on the River Tigris near to Mosul in present day Iraq. So the various prophets didn't just preach to the Jews but also to the Gentiles.

Simeon in the Temple said of Jesus (Luke ch 2 v 30-32) 'For my eyes have seen Thy salvation, which you have prepared in the sight of all people, a light for a revelation to the Gentiles and for glory to your people Israel'. And in Luke ch 4 Jesus refers to the times when Elijah and Elisha visited Gentile people.

Let's get back to Jonah. He was called by God to go to preach to the people of Nineveh but he refused to go. He went down to the coast to a port called Joppa and paid his fare to go as far away from Nineveh as possible. Where did he want to go? To a place called Tarshish, and where was Tarshish? Spain. Nipping off to Spain is not just a present day idea. We read all kinds of criminals are to be found in Spain. Was it the same in Jonah's time? He just wanted to go as far away as possible.

So the ship set sail from Joppa, but it wasn't going to be a holiday for Jonah. Immediately, the wind blew up a violent storm. Even the sailors were scared and they started to throw cargo overboard to lighten the ship. What would you have done if you had been on board? Jonah went below and fell into a deep sleep.

The captain must have known a bit about Jonah as he personally went below deck to wake him. 'How can you sleep? Call on your God, maybe He'll save us.' The sailors had an idea which was common in the middle East, 'Let's cast lots to see who is responsible for this calamity.' I don't think Jonah was surprised when the lot fell on him.

There are several examples in Scripture of people casting lots to discover the will of God, even up to Acts ch 1 v 23-26. Casting the lots was accompanied by prayer. Why don't we do this today? Of course, many people do - the lottery! But, in the Christian church, casting lots has not been used since the coming of the Holy Spirit.

Back to Jonah - well the lot fell on Jonah and the sailors asked Jonah what they should do. 'Throw me into the sea.' They needed some persuasion but they obeyed and peace was restored and they acknowledged Jonah's God.

Now what happened? Jonah was swallowed by a great fish. Inside the great fish, Jonah prayed. He was having second thoughts and lo and behold, the fish (excuse the expression) threw him up on to dry land. Again, God called Jonah to go to Nineveh and this time, he obeyed. He preached and the people of Nineveh repented and were saved from terrible destruction.

Before we continue with Jonah's adventures., let's pause. Do you really believe that Jonah was swallowed by a great fish and was then thrown up on to a beach?

D.W.B. Robinson offers some thoughts on this problem:

(i) Jonah was an historical figure, a prophet, son of Amittai serving King Jeroboam II.
(ii) The book of Jonah is an historical record and up to recent years has been accepted as such by both Jewish and Christian scholars. In more recent days, some scholars appear to be losing belief in anything.
(iii) In Matthew ch 12 v 38-41, Jesus clearly believed that the people of Nineveh repented after the preaching of Jonah and Jesus compares His own stay in the grave for three days in a similar way.

There will always be people who will try to explain away the miracles recorded in the Bible. To repeat myself, if we believe in Genesis ch 1 v 1, then God can do anything. If He made the Heavens and the earth and what other explanation is there, God can do anything. And He can do anything for you.

But, we are not yet at the end of the story. Why didn't Jonah want to go to Nineveh? Was he afraid? What was wrong with Nineveh? Listen to this. Ch. 4 v 1. Jonah did not want to go to Nineveh because he knew the Lord was going to have compassion on the residents. Can you believe this? Jonah had the sulks because the Lord had compassion on more than 120,000 people. The Lord said, 'Should I not be concerned about that great city?' Let's be honest, do we ever behave like that? Do we ever want to rain down judgement on others?

The story of Jonah contains many lessons. (i) The lesson of obedience. It is so difficult for us to do as we are told. Is there something that the Lord is demanding from you or me just now? We pray for guidance and courage to do what we should. (ii) Compassion. It's strange that Nineveh was saved by a reluctant prophet. Except I am moved with compassion, how dwelleth Thy Spirit in me?

Chapter 40
For Thine is the Kingdom

For Thine is the Kingdom, and the Power and the Glory for ever and ever. Amen

Some scholars will tell us that this sentence (Doxology) was not originally part of the Lord's Prayer. Indeed, when we read the N.I.V. translation, we find that these words have been omitted - they have gone!

Apparently, these words were included by and came into use during the early days of the Christian Church and we have carried on the practice ever since. These words are included in the A.V. but not in more modern versions. So, do we have a problem? Where do these words come from? Are they scriptural?

They certainly are. The early church took the phrases from the Old Testament, we find them in 2 Chronicles ch 29 v 11. So, the early church has condensed these words, which we call a doxology - a formula of praise to God - and concluded the Lord's Prayer with a final hymn of praise. I don't know about you, but I would miss this conclusion. Have you been to a church service where they have been omitted? For us, the prayer does not seem to have ended correctly. But, what do these words mean?

For Thine is the Kingdom.

What does the word Kingdom conjure up in your mind? (Any offers?) I, initially, think of a fairy tale where there is a palace, surrounded by a small town, surrounded by a high wall to keep the dragon out. There is a king and queen, a beautiful princess and from another place, a handsome prince wanting the hand of the princess, which he can have - after he has slain the dragon! There are more similarities in that story to real life than at first seems.

Earlier in the Lord's prayer, we pray 'Thy Kingdom come'. When we read our papers and listen to or see the news, we know without any doubt whatsoever that God's Kingdom has not yet been established. The terrible things that happen somewhere everyday are well documented. Someone has said 'Everything seems to have a crack in it' Thy Kingdom come is a trumpet call for us to play our part in the world of today. But, we must always keep in mind that God's Kingdom WILL come.

Jesus preached the Kingdom of Heaven - particularly in St. Matthew's gospel, look up ch 13: The Kingdom of Heaven is like - a man who sowed good seed in his field....is like a mustard seed....is like yeast...is like treasure hid in a field....is like a merchant looking for fine pearls. The Kingdom of Heaven will come. That is why Jesus came. He came to slay the dragon of sin, pain. evil and death. 'In the world you will have trouble. But take heart! I have overcome the world.'

For Thine IS the Kingdom for ever and ever.

For Thine is the Power.

What picture does power conjure up? Wind, sea (a TV programme looked into the problem of freak waves.

Apparently, ships are built on a formula that includes the belief that a freak wave happens once in 10,000 years. They have recently discovered that the formula is false. The world's largest and 'safest' tanker is no match against a freak wave). Earthquakes, volcanoes? We think of the greatest empires Persian, Greek, Roman, Nazis, Communists… Where are they now?

We have all seen evidence of power in one way or another, if not in reality on T.V. The power on men, mechanical, in war, atomic power, rocket power. We have seen the power of nature, waterfalls, the sea, volcanoes, the sun. How did the sun and the stars get up there? Our knowledge of the universe is so limited. A starry night displays the Glory of God and His Power. Genesis ch 1 v 1 'In the beginning, God created the heavens and the earth…' Dr. Campbell Morgan said something like if God created the heavens and the earth, why should we be surprised that Jesus rose from the dead? He can do anything. Job ch 26 v 14 'Who then can understand the thunder of His power?' I think we can say, 'We've seen nothing yet'.

For Thine is the Glory.

What picture does glory conjure up? 50,000 fans celebrating a win in a cup final? Just think of it West Ham 10 Manchester United 0. We are trying to imagine something worthy of praise, exaltation, honour, adoration. In life anything, the best of our imagination is just a fleeting moment, transient, temporary, passing. 'Change and decay is all around I see, O Thou who changest not, abide with me.' I think sometimes, we have to remind ourselves that Our God is all knowing, everywhere present, all powerful -and we are His children. Your weakness, your problems, your sin, your inadequacies, your fears and worries can be taken up by Our Father God and sorted. Nothing on earth can meet or answer our deepest needs - certainly not money, fame, drugs, alcohol, nor even education.

For Thine is the Kingdom and the Power and the Glory for ever and ever. Amen.
Christ is the answer.

2 Corinthians ch 4 v 16-18.

Chapter 41
Epitaphs, etc.

A vicar noticed a dead donkey lying in a field near his church, left behind by a group of campers. He phoned the local council to report the matter. The council official said waggishly that he thought that it was the duty of the vicar to bury the dead. 'That may be,' replied the vicar, 'but I thought the least I could do was to inform the next of kin.'

A Yorkshireman's wife died and he commissioned a headstone with the simple inscription 'She was Thine'. A little later he was informed that the stone was ready for inspection. He noticed immediately that there was a mistake for the stone read 'She was thin.' He rang the mason and complained 'You've left the E off.' Many apologies were offered and the mason promised that the stone would be corrected as soon as possible. In time, the mason called to say all was well, the stone was done. The Yorkshireman visited the cemetery and read the inscription, 'E she was thin'.

At one time, film stars began to write their own epitaphs:
W.C. Fields: 'On the whole I'd rather be in Philadelphia.'
Lionel Barrymore: 'Well I've played everything but the harp.'
Clark Gable: 'Back to the silents.'
Frederic March: 'This is just my lot.'
Warner Baxter. 'Did you hear about my operation.'

Spike Milligan suggested 'I told you I was ill.'

Here are a few more actual examples:

After a sad shooting accident:
Sacred to the memory of Major James Bush who was killed by accidental discharge of a pistol by his orderly. 14 April 1831. Well done thou good and faithful servant.

Sudden and unexpected was the end of our esteemed and beloved friend. He gave all his friends a sudden shock by one day falling into Sunderland dock.

Erected to the memory of John Macfarlane, drowned in the Water of Leith by a few of his affectionate friends.

Here lies the body of Samuel Young who came here and died for the benefit of his health.

Here lies my wife, here let her lie, now she's at rest, and so am I.

Finally, like Spike's earlier, a notorious hypochondriac had one word 'See'.

This seems a strange subject to laugh about (especially for the English) but just this week a friend in the church paid tribute to his mother at her funeral. His wife said, 'You should have heard Roger. He had them all laughing.' This is not strange for the Christian who should have no fear of death.

Sir John Lawrence attended what he describes as a sort of Communist Memorial Service to Stanislavsky, famous Russian actor in the Moscow Arts Theatre. He writes.' .....One heard some of the world's greatest actors speaking of their teacher and leader on what should have been a moving occasion, but the experience was empty. I was not at that time a Christian believer but it struck me that Communism has nothing to say about death.' Similarly, Bertrand Russell says, 'Brief and powerless is man's life; on his and all his race, the slow sure doom falls pitiless and dark...' Humanism has also nothing to say.

In his recent autobiography, John Gowans, a former general in the Salvation Army,-tells the story of a visit to one of his soldiers in Liverpool. The lady in question was full of love and compassion. She made a point of comforting the bereaved in her area. On entering her living room, John noticed three smart military men in photos on the mantel piece and asked who they were. 'Oh, they are my three boys. They were all killed in the last war.' And she hurried into the kitchen to make a cup of tea......

Jesus said, 'I am the Resurrection and the Life., he who believes in Me, though he die, yet shall he live and whoever lives and believes in Me shall never die.'

Lightning Source UK Ltd.
Milton Keynes UK
UKHW02f0123180818
327368UK00006B/406/P